THE

CHRONOLOGY

OF EZRA 7

Second Edition, Revised

SIEGFRIED H. HORN

and

LYNN H. WOOD

•

TEACH Services, Inc.

www.TEACHServices.com

Facsimile Reproduction

As this book played a formative role in the development of Christian thought and the publisher feels that this book, with its candor and depth, still holds significance for the church today. Therefore the publisher has chosen to reproduce this historical classic from an original copy. Frequent variations in the quality of the print are unavoidable due to the condition of the original. Thus the print may look darker or lighter or appear to be missing detail, more in some places than in others.

Copyright © 2006 TEACH Services, Inc.
ISBN-13: 9781479616220
Library of Congress Control Number: 2006926246

Published by

TEACH Services, Inc.
www.TEACHServices.com

Preface

THE PROBLEMS connected with the dating of Artaxerxes I of Persia have long intrigued Biblical historians because the 7th and 20th regnal years of that king are mentioned in the Bible in connection with important events in the history of Israel, yet these events have been given differing B.C. dates in different works.

Among those studying this problem was Lynn H. Wood, for many years professor of archeology and history of antiquity at the Seventh-day Adventist Theological Seminary (at that time situated in Washington, D.C.). Over a period of several years he built up a considerable body of materials concerning the principles, methods, and theories of Hebrew and other ancient chronology and calendation bearing on the problems involved in the present work. He made a study of the correlation between the Egyptian and non-Egyptian dates in the double-dated Jewish papyri from Elephantine which led eventually to satisfactory solutions in the area of ancient Jewish calendation, especially of the period of Artaxerxes. He also laid down principles and indicated directions that further research should take.

Siegfried H. Horn, a former student of Wood and, after the latter's retirement, his successor in the Seminary (now part of Andrews University, Berrien Springs,

3

Michigan), followed his tutor's leads and methods.

The discovery of the Brooklyn Museum Aramaic papyri (published by Kraeling in 1953)—an additional group of double-dated fifth-century papyri from Elephantine—led to the writing of the present work. Although Horn wrote the book (with the able assistance of Julia Neuffer of the Review and Herald Publishing Association), the name of L. H. Wood appears quite properly on the title page as coauthor.

The first edition, published in 1953, was exhausted some years ago, and since then there has been a steady stream of demands for a reprint of this technical work on ancient chronology. However, new discoveries of documents and a re-evaluation of old material have called for a revision, which in some sections has amounted to considerable rewriting. The new source material, especially, for example, the Babylonian chronicle published in 1956 by D. J. Wiseman, has been incorporated as far as it has a bearing on the subject.

Several additional appendixes have been inserted, which deal with special phases of the subject: Ptolemy's Canon with an added column giving the Julian date of Thoth 1 in each 1st year; extracts from and discussions of the sources related to the Xerxes-Artaxerxes transition; and a lunar-calendar table based on the dating of the Elephantine papyri.

This book is now published the second time in the hope that it will clarify the subject further and once more make a contribution to the solution of a somewhat difficult problem in Biblical chronology.

4

Contents

Tables and Illustrations

5

List of Abbreviations

AJSL	= *The American Journal of Semitic Languages and Literatures.*
AP 1, 2, etc.	= Papyri in Cowley, A. *Aramaic Papyri of the Fifth Century B.C.*
AUSS	= *Andrews University Seminary Studies.*
BASOR	= *Bulletin of the American Schools of Oriental Research.*
CAH	= *The Cambridge Ancient History.*
JNES	= *Journal of Near Eastern Studies.*
Kraeling 1, 2, etc.	= Papyri in Kraeling, Emil G. *The Brooklyn Museum Aramaic Papyri.*
LBART	= *Late Babylonian Astronomical and Related Texts,* ed. by A. J. Sachs.
sr-sr	= Sunrise to sunrise.
ss-ss	= Sunset to sunset.

Introduction

THE PURPOSE of this study is to examine the date of Ezra's journey from Babylon to Palestine in the 7th regnal year of Artaxerxes. In the 18th and 19th centuries many writers on Bible history dated this event in 457 B.C., though some held 458 and a few 467. This variation was due to the differing methods of chronologists in their attempts to apply, adapt, or revise the data in the ancient chronological sources, principally Ptolemy's Canon.

The date 457 was the favorite choice among the 19th-century Biblical expositors who placed in the time of Ezra and Nehemiah the starting point of the 2300 prophetic days of Daniel 8 or of the seventy-week period of Daniel 9, which from "the going forth of the commandment to restore and to build Jerusalem" was to reach until the ministry of the Messiah. Probably the larger number who were more interested in the Biblical than the technical factors were influenced by the date 457 in the margin of Ezra 7 in the King James Bibles. This figure was the result of a revision of James Ussher's date (467) by William Lloyd, who in 1701 introduced Ussher's B.C. dating into the marginal notes. "Ussher" dates, appearing in K.J.V. printings for more than 200 years, were regarded in mid-19th century as "the received chronology," or even "the Bible chronology."

However, before the end of the century many Bible

helps and commentaries, even those retaining the old marginal 457, presented 458 for Ezra's journey to Jerusalem in the 7th year of Artaxerxes, deriving the date from historical works that used Ptolemy's Canon (Egyptian) year, 459/58. In recent decades 458 has been based on the Babylonian-Persian year 458/57, as a result of a greater knowledge of ancient history and chronology through the discovery of ancient documents. These records have provided accurate dates for many events that took place during the Persian empire period and in general have also placed the reigns of the Persian kings on a secure basis.

During the past hundred years tens of thousands of original documents have been unearthed, many of which bear witness to events recorded by classical historians, and some to events recorded in the Bible. The study of ancient chronology has especially benefited by these discoveries, with the result that the chronologies of early Egypt and Mesopotamia now rest on a much more secure foundation than they did only a few decades ago. The chronologies of these same countries during the first millennium B.C. have become so nearly accurate that differences of interpretation provide dates that are seldom more than one year apart. To mention examples, the Battle of Qarqar between Shalmaneser III of Assyria and a coalition of ten western allies is dated by most scholars in 853 B.C. and by a minority in 854; the destruction of Jerusalem by Nebuchadnezzar is dated by many Biblical historians in 586, but by others in 587 B.C., and the fall of Samaria is dated on the basis of some ancient evidence in 723, but on the basis of other evidence in 722 B.C. Our own study deals with an event where differences of interpretation have resulted in dates that are also one year apart, as has already been stated.

Hand in hand with the advance in chronological and historical knowledge resulting from the discoveries of the documentary material is an increased understanding of ancient calendars and dating systems. This has been obtained through dated business documents, such as contracts, deeds, receipts, and others, written either on clay tablets in Babylonia or on papyri in Egypt, occasionally even engraved in stone. The result has been that many obscure and uncertain points of chronology, calendation, time reckoning, and dating systems have been cleared up.

The reader will see by the evidence provided in the present book that a date is derived not only from adding up certain years of an era or of a king list but also from a number of other factors, such as (1) a correct understanding of the calendar employed by the ancient people whose documents are used as the basis of computations; (2) a familiarity with the methods of dating, which may be entirely different from our own; and (3) taking into account the fact that systems of reckoning time occasionally changed.

In order to proceed from the known to the unknown, let us begin with a look at our own dating system. The month names January, February, March, and so on, are Roman, and the 365-day year was introduced

9

into Europe from Egypt by Julius Caesar, who added the leap-year feature. This "Julian" calendar, inherited by the nations which succeeded the Roman empire, has come down to us in a slightly corrected form called the "Gregorian" calendar. This, along with the B.C.-A.D. system of year numbering, originating in medieval times, has spread over the globe with the European expansion until it has become familiar even in remote countries that have entirely different calendars of their own.

Thus a large part of the world today is accustomed, not only to the dating of modern happenings in terms of the Gregorian calendar and the Christian era, but also to the historical dating of all ancient events as if the Julian calendar and the B.C. scale of years extended backward indefinitely into the remote past. We say, for example, that Jerusalem fell to Nebuchadnezzar in 586 B.C., that Cyrus died in August, 530 B.C., and that Alexander the Great died in June, 323 B.C. Having become accustomed to such a system of dating, we find it hard to realize that the original records from which we learn about these and other ancient events are given in various dating systems quite different from ours.

Let us briefly review the evidence for the three mentioned dates and see how each one is based on chronological evidence different from the others. For the fall of Jerusalem we have the Bible statements dating it in the 19th year of Nebuchadnezzar and the 11th year of Zedekiah. Nebuchadnezzar's 19th year happens to be more easily located than many others, because archeologists have found a document from the time of Nebuchadnezzar giving a series of astronomical observations for his 37th year that locate that B.C. year unmistakably, and therefore also the 19th year. However, we must also know the relationship between Nebuchadnezzar's Babylonian years and Zedekiah's Jewish years in order to be sure of the date for the fall of the city. For the death of Cyrus the Great we have Ptolemy's Canon and a contemporary eclipse record which necessitate placing the first year of his successor, Cambyses, in the spring of 529 B.C., following Cyrus' 9th Persian year. Other Babylonian tablets indicate the time of year at which his reign ended. For Alexander's death a record exists that dates the event in the 1st year of the 114th Olympiad, a Greek dating used in the classical period.

Such various types of dating formulas in different calendars, often more variable and less exact than the ones mentioned, must be pieced together by careful and sometimes laborious methods in order to date ancient events. Some can be located exactly in the B.C. scheme of dating, and others only approximately.

The necessity of understanding these problems becomes obvious when we consider the case of the historical events connected with the starting point of the prophetic 2300-day period: Ezra's journey to Jerusalem lasting from the 1st to the 5th month of "the seventh year" of the reign of Artaxerxes. The date is given in terms of a regnal year of a Persian ruler as reckoned by a Jew from Babylon who was writing for Palestinian

11

Jews about events connected with Palestine. In order to assign these events with certainty to a B.C. date, we must answer a number of questions: What did Ezra mean by the 1st and the 5th month, and what kind of calendar did he use? What did he mean by dating his return to Jerusalem in the 7th year of the reign of King Artaxerxes? Did he reckon it from the date of accession or by calendar years? If the latter, did he use Persian or Jewish years, and if Jewish, which of the systems known to have been used by the Jews? Such varied elements enter into the problem of locating ancient events in the B.C.-A.D. scale. Therefore the first four chapters will be devoted to a basic explanation of the necessary facts about ancient dating methods that are essential for a correct interpretation of Biblical dates in general and those connected with the 2300-day prophetic period in particular.

A careful study of the first two chapters is therefore indispensable for an understanding of chapters 3 to 5 dealing with the specific problems of the Jewish calendar and the chronology of Ezra 7, and Appendix 2 presents a detailed discussion of some extra-Biblical Jewish documents of the 5th century B.C. by which the correctness of the conclusions reached in chapter 5 is established. For an understanding of the solution of the problem discussed, a reading of Appendix 2 is not essential, but this material is included for those who want to have all the evidence on which our knowledge of the Jewish calendar of the 5th century B.C. is based.

CHAPTER ONE

Different Dating Systems

IN THE Bible, and in other records of ancient nations, various methods are used to date events. The most ancient records of Mesopotamia reveal that economic reasons were responsible for the invention of systems by which time could be fixed; for instance, to determine how much rent had to be paid for the loan of an animal for a certain period of time, or for the rent of a house, et cetera. However, the ancients did not know how to reckon time according to an era, as we moderns are accustomed to doing, an era that has a fixed point of departure (as the birth of Christ in the Christian era), and that numbers consecutively each year without regard for events.

Lists of Year Names

The earliest known way of fixing a chronology, as practiced by the ancient Sumerians and Babylonians, was to give a name to each year, the name of the most conspicuous event of the previous year. In this way the 7th year of Hammurabi, for example, was called the "year Uruk and Isin were taken," and the 10th year of his reign was called the "year the army and people of Malgu were destroyed," although in both cases the

13

actual events referred to had happened in the respective preceding years.[1] In the various offices and cities were kept complete lists of all year names covering a reasonable period, so that it could be determined how many years had passed if a man claimed, for instance, that someone owed him rent for a piece of land from the "year Uruk and Isin were taken" to the "year the army and people of Malgu were destroyed." From such lists it could be determined that between the two aforementioned years lay the two following ones: (1) the "year the land of Emutbal (was?) [destroyed]," and (2) the "year the canal Hammurabi-hegal (was dug)." Although such reckoning of time seems very cumbersome to us moderns, who without a moment's hesitation know how many years lie between 1950 and 1953, this reckoning according to year names was practiced for many centuries in Mesopotamia.

Eponym Canons

Another method of fixing years was introduced by the Assyrians. A high official, including the king, was appointed once during his life, to serve for one year as *limmu,* which was an honorary office requiring the performance of no duties, but merely giving his name to the year in which he was *limmu.* The Greek equivalent of the Assyrian *limmu* is the word "eponym";

---

[1] The examples of all year names are taken from Samuel A. B. Mercer, *Sumero-Babylonian Year-Formulae,* pp. 35, 36. The proof that years were named after events of the *previous* year, and not after events of the current year, was provided by a tablet in the Peiser collection. It was published by Ernst Weidner, "Zur altbabylonischen Jahresbenennung," *Orientalistische Literaturzeitung,* 15 (1912), cols. 392, 393.

hence the chronological lists containing the names of the *limmu* are called Eponym Canons.[2] Thus we find in the year when King Sargon II came to the throne an eponym by the name Nimurta-ilaia, and all the documents were dated during that year in "the year Nimurta-ilaia." This eponym was followed the next year by Nabu-taris, and every dated document bore the entry "the year Nabu-taris."[3] Lists of the eponyms, like the lists of the year names in early Babylonia, had to be kept for business or legal purposes. This system of time reckoning was employed by the Assyrians from about 2000 B.C. to the end of the empire's existence in the late 7th century B.C.

Regnal Years

In Egypt dating was done, from the earliest historical times, according to years of the reign of each king, called regnal years. This system was also introduced in Babylonia by the Kassite rulers in the middle of the second millennium B.C. Since this form of time reckoning is the one encountered in the documents, Biblical and extra-Biblical, with which this study is concerned, this system has to be explained in somewhat greater detail than the previously mentioned systems, which have no bearing on the subject under discussion.

To the average person today the expression "first

---

[2] A. Ungnad. "Eponymen," *Reallexikon der Assyriologie*, vol. 2 (1938), pp. 412-457; see also Sidney Smith, "The Foundation of the Assyrian Empire," and "The Age of Ashurbanipal," in *The Cambridge Ancient History* (hereinafter abbreviated to *CAH*), vol. 3, pp. 3, 92, 93.

[3] Ungnad, *op. cit.*, p. 424; Daniel D. Luckenbill, *Ancient Records of Assyria and Babylonia*, vol. 2, p. 437.

year of Darius" would naturally mean the first twelve months of his reign, beginning from the date of his accession to the throne. Indeed, in this way—counting by anniversaries of the accession—the years of the British rulers are reckoned, and by such regnal years the laws, until recently, were dated.[4] But in everyday life it is more convenient to date by calendar years that always begin on the same date and are numbered by a long-term scale, like the Christian era.

During the period of the Babylonian and Persian kings with which the first part of this study deals, formulas such as the following are found: "in the month Nisan, in the twentieth year of Artaxerxes the king" (Neh. 2:1). But the ancients had two methods by which they avoided the troubles inherent in counting years by each ruler's anniversaries. Disregarding the varying dates of the actual accessions, they reckoned all reigns so as to make the regnal year coincide with the calendar year. The difference between the two methods by which this was done was in the treatment of the interval between the day of a king's accession to the throne and the next New Year's Day.

Accession-year reckoning (postdating).—Under the accession-year system of counting regnal years the unexpired portion of the calendar year in which a king's reign begins is called his accession year. Then his first full year, coinciding with the next calendar year, is numbered "year 1." The Assyrians, the Babylonians, and the Persians after them, used the accession-

---

[4] Frederick C. Hicks, *Materials and Methods of Legal Research*, p. 430.

year system.[5] Some of the Hebrew kings also employed it, as can be determined by synchronisms between the years of contemporary kings of Israel and Judah.

To illustrate this method, let us suppose that a Babylonian king (A) dies in the 5th month of the 20th year of his reign, and is succeeded by his son (B). Archeologists have found dated contracts, letters, and other documents, written on clay tablets, covering this period. The documents of the first five months, up to the time of the king's death, are dated in the 20th year of King A. But a receipt, let us say, signed in the 6th month, will be dated "in the 6th month of the accession year [literally "the beginning of kingship"][6] of King B." During all the rest of that calendar year the scribes will be dating documents in the accession year of the new king. Then on the first day of the new year they change to a date formula which reads, "in the 1st month of the year 1 of King B."[7] The use of the designation "year 1" has been deferred until the New Year's Day following the accession.

This system, often called postdating because the beginning of the 1st regnal year is being postponed, makes the regnal years coincide with the calendar years,

---

[5] See Richard A. Parker and Waldo H. Dubberstein, *Babylonian Chronology, 626 B.C.-A.D. 75* (1956), pp. 10-19.

[6] Arno Poebel, "The Duration of the Reign of Smerdis, the Magian, and the Reigns of Nebuchadnezzar III and Nebuchadnezzar IV," *The American Journal of Semitic Languages and Literatures* (hereinafter abbreviated to *AJSL*), 56 (1939), p. 121.

[7] For the Nisan beginning of the regnal years, see the sequence of the observation dates in an astronomical text of the time of Nebuchadnezzar, in Paul V. Neugebauer and Ernst F. Weidner, "Ein astronomischer Beobachtungstext aus dem 37. Jahre Nebukadnezars II. (-567/66) [i.e. 568/67 B.C.]," *Berichte über die Verhandlungen der Königl. Sächsischen Gesellschaft der Wissenschaften zu Leipzig*, Phil.-Hist. Klasse, 67 (1915), part 2, pp. 34, 38.

and avoids giving two numbers to the year in which the accession takes place. Thus the calendar year which has begun as the 20th of the father is followed by the year 1 of the son. The distinguishing mark of this system is the term "accession year," applied to the interval lying between the accession of a king and the first New Year's Day, after which his nominal 1st year begins.

Non-accession-year   reckoning   (antedating).— The opposite method of counting regnal years, employed at times in Egypt,[8] and also indicated in the Bible, has no "accession-year" designation. Documents written in the unexpired portion of King A's last year begin immediately to be dated in King B's "year 1," and on the first New Year's Day the dating changes to the year 2 of the reign. This method has the disadvantage of causing an overlap in numbering, a double dating for the year in which the reigns change, for that year bears the last number of the old king and also the number 1 of the new one. This system is often called antedating.

Therefore, if the same reign is reckoned by different chroniclers using the two systems—as is sometimes the case in the records of Judah and Israel[9]—the year numbers as recorded in the accession-year system will run a year later than those reckoned according to the non-accession-year system, as Figure 1 will show.

---

[8] Richard A. Parker, "Persian and Egyptian Chronology," *AJSL*, 58 (1941), pp. 298, 299.

[9] See Edwin R. Thiele, *The Mysterious Numbers of the Hebrew Kings*, pp. 22-27.

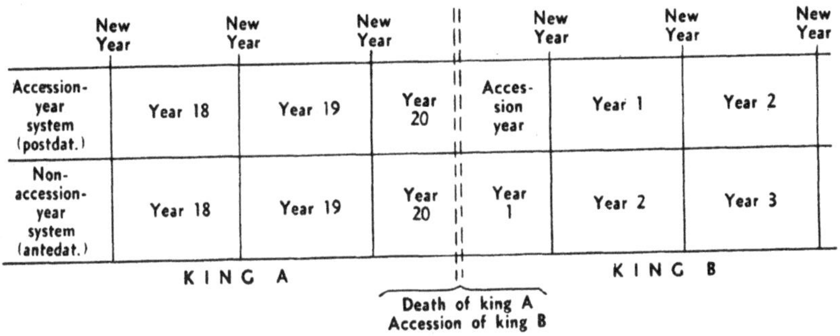

	New Year	New Year	New Year			New Year	New Year	New Year
Accession-year system (postdat.)	Year 18	Year 19	Year 20		Accession year	Year 1	Year 2	
Non-accession-year system (antedat.)	Year 18	Year 19	Year 20		Year 1	Year 2	Year 3	
	KING A					KING B		

Death of king A
Accession of king B

Fig. 1

Further, it should be noted that in totaling a list of reigns reckoned according to the accession-year system the sum of years recorded for each king is the same as the actual number of years elapsed, whereas in adding a succession of reigns reckoned according to the non-accession-year system, a year must be subtracted for each king, because the last year of one reign and the first of the next are really the same.

In dealing with Biblical records, it is necessary to know in each case which of these two regnal systems is used—the accession- or non-accession-year systems.

A clear case of reckoning a king's regnal years according to the accession-year system is given in 2 Kings 18:1, 9, 10. After having stated that Hezekiah came to the throne in the 3d year of Hoshea, the writer declares that the siege of Samaria began in the 4th year of Hezekiah, which was the 7th year of Hoshea, and ended three years later in the 6th year of Hezekiah, which was the 9th year of Hoshea. The two possible reckonings of Hezekiah's reign would give the following results:

1. According to the non-accession-year system (antedating):

Year 1 of Hezekiah - - Year 3 of Hoshea
Year 2 "   "   - - Year 4 "   "
Year 3 "   "   - - Year 5 "   "
Year 4 "   "   - - Year 6 "   "
Year 5 "   "   - - Year 7 "   "
Year 6 "   "   - - Year 8 "   "

2. According to the accession-year system (postdating):

Accession year of Hezekiah Year 3 of Hoshea
Year 1   "   "   - Year 4 "   "
Year 2   "   "   - Year 5 "   "
Year 3   "   "   - Year 6 "   "
Year 4   "   "   - Year 7 "   "
Year 5   "   "   - Year 8 "   "
Year 6   "   "   - Year 9 "   "

From this it can be easily seen that Hezekiah must have used an accession-year system. On the other hand, a clear example of non-accession-year reckoning is the reign of Nadab of Israel, who came to the throne in the 2d year of Asa of Judah. Nadab reigned two years, and was killed in the 3d year of Asa (1 Kings 15:25, 28). The two possible reckonings of his reign would run thus:

1. According to the accession-year system (postdating):

Accession year of Nadab Year 2 of Asa (latter part)
Year 1   "   "   Year 3 "   "
Year 2   "   "   Year 4 "   "

20

2. According to the non-accession-year system (antedating):

Year 1 of Nadab - - Year 2 of Asa (latter part)
Year 2 "   "   - - Year 3 "   "

Obviously the non-accession-year system, and not the other, fits the record; for after having come to the throne in Asa's 2d year, the king reigned two years—that is, his death occurred in his 2d year—and died in the 3d year of Asa. A chronicler who recorded Nadab's accession in the 2d year of Asa could not consistently have given him an "accession year," a "year 1," and a "year 2," in two consecutive years. There are other similar examples of non-accession-year reckoning in the Bible.[10] These examples and others that could be cited show that the Hebrews used both systems at different times.[11]

It is necessary to know which system is involved if a regnal date of any king is to be located in the B.C. scale of the Julian calendar. This is so because, even if the exact B.C. date of a king's accession is known, his regnal-year numbering will run one year later if reckoning is made according to the postdating or accession-year system than if it is done according to the antedating or non-accession-year system. These differences between the types of regnal-year reckoning in

---

[10] See 1 Kings 16:8, 10; 22:40, 51; 2 Kings 1:1, 2, 17; 3:1. A supposed difficulty in reckoning twelve years from Ahab to Jehu, spanning 2 intervening reigns of 2 years plus 12 years, is cleared up by the application of this method. See S. A. Cook, "Chronology: II. The Old Testament," *CAH*, vol. 1, chap. 4, sec. 2, p. 160.

[11] See Thiele, *op. cit.*, pp. 34-38.

relation to the accession date must be understood in order to interpret correctly the dated source documents of the reigns of Xerxes and Artaxerxes. Three other types of year numbering, less important to the problem than the contemporary regnal-year datings, have been used by later writers in connection with the accession of Artaxerxes—the Greek archonships and Olympiads and the Roman consular dating.[12]

Archon List

Among the Greeks the various city states had no more uniformity in their respective calendars than they had political unity. The Athenians designated each year by the name of the archon, or chief magistrate, for that year.[13] They used their archon list as the Assyrians used their Eponym Canon to date events, and so did Greek historians elsewhere, like Diodorus of Sicily.

There was a difference, however, between the eponymous archon of Athens and the *limmu* of Assyria: The archon was always a titular head of state, but the *limmu* could be any of various officials and dignitaries of the Assyrian Empire, for whom the office of eponym was an honorary one.

---

[12] Diodorus Siculus (xi. 69; Loeb ed., vol. 4, p. 305) places the death of Xerxes in the year when Lysitheüs was archon in Athens and the two consuls elected at Rome were Lucius Valerius Publicola and Titus Aemilius Mamercus. Eusebius in his *Chronicle* (4th century A.D.) places it in the 4th year of the 78th Olympiad, 465/64 B.C., midsummer to midsummer (see p. 167, note 15). Diodorus' consular date does not harmonize with the other known dates, but the Olympiad date and the archonship of Lysitheüs agree with what is known from other chronological sources. For the date of the archonship of Lysitheüs, see F. K. Ginzel, *Handbuch der mathematischen und technischen Chronologie*, vol. 2, p. 587, Tafel VI.

[13] E. A. Gardner and M. Cary, "Early Athens," in *CAH*, vol. 3, pp. 590-593; on the archon lists see also William Bell Dinsmoor, *The Archons of Athens in the Hellenistic Age*.

DIFFERENT DATING SYSTEMS

Olympiads

Besides the Athenian scheme of reckoning, there was another, used by all the Greeks—the Olympiads, the four-year periods between the Olympic games. The sacred festival at Olympia, celebrated once every four years, was the one occasion when all the Greek states put aside their feuds and united in joyous celebration. Thus the dating of the Olympic games was important to all, and eventually the practice arose of dating an event in a certain year of a certain Olympiad. It should be noted that the 1st year of the 1st Olympiad is 776/5 B.C., from midsummer to midsummer,[14] since, traditionally, the first Olympic games were held in the summer of 776 B.C. The fact that this date is only traditional[15] does not impair the usefulness of the chronological scale any more than the error of a few years in the actual birth date of Christ affects the value of the Christian era for dating purposes. Olympiad dating was used by Greek and Roman classical writers, and also by Josephus. The formula "in the 4th year of the 85th Olympiad" is sometimes abbreviated to Ol. 85. 4.

Consular List

The Romans most often used for dating purposes the method of designating the year by the names of

---

[14] The double date 776/75 is given here to call attention to the fact that the Olympiad years and all ancient calendar years (except the Roman, which we still use) overlap parts of two of our present calendar years. The practice of writing such double dates as 776/75, which is becoming more common, is the only sure way of avoiding errors in expressing the B.C. equivalents of ancient calendar years.

[15] For theories about the dating of the Olympiads, see H. T. Wade-Gery, Chronological Note 3 on "Olympic Victor Lists," in *CAH*, vol. 3, pp. 762-764, *cf.* table, p. 767.

the two consuls, the highest Roman officials, appointed annually by the Senate.[16] "In the consulship of Lepidus and Arruntius"—literally "Lepidus and Arruntius being consuls"—was the official Roman formula, although in the time of the empire the eastern provinces applied their older regnal-year system also to the emperors.[17] In the later Roman period Fasti, or lists of officials, including the consuls [18] became standard chronological scales like the archon list of Athens.

Era of the Foundation of Rome

The Romans also developed a true historical era beginning with the traditional founding of the city, generally placed at 753 B.C.[19] This reckoning *ab urbe condita,* or *anno urbis conditae,* abbreviated to A.U.C., is sometimes counted from April 21, which came to be celebrated as the birthday of Rome,[20] though at times from January 1, the beginning of the ordinary Roman calendar.[21] It was used less often for dating purposes than the consulship formula. Although the era ran the-

---

[16] H. Stuart Jones and Hugh Last, "The Early Republic," in *CAH,* vol. 7, p. 437.

[17] An example is the date formula of Luke 3:1—"in the fifteenth year of the reign of Tiberius Caesar."

[18] The *Chronographus Anni CCCLIIII* contains one of these consular lists, entitled "Fasti Consulares," published in *Chronica Minora Saec. IV. V. VI. VII.,* ed. Theodor Mommsen, vol. 1 ("Monumenta Germaniae Historica," Auct. Ant. vol. 9), pp. 50-61.

[19] Roman historians differed in dating the founding of Rome, but the year most commonly accepted is from Varro, who lived in the first century B.C. See H. Stuart Jones, "The Sources for the Tradition of Early Roman History," in *CAH,* vol. 7, pp. 321, 322, and table.

[20] This was the festival of the Parilia, or Palilia. See Censorinus, *De Die Natale* ("The Natal Day"), chap. 10 (21), trans. William Maude, p. 32.

[21] Among other eras the current year A.U.C., reckoned from January 1, appears every year in *The American Ephemeris and Nautical Almanac.*

oretically from 753 B.C., it was not the oldest continuous era in length of use.

The Seleucid Era

One of the first eras actually used was that of the Seleucids, which was widely found throughout the Near East during the last three pre-Christian centuries. It began with Seleucus I's reign, reckoned from 312 B.C., and its years were continuously counted through—at least in some Eastern countries outside the Roman Empire—until the first Christian century. In the Macedonian calendar the years of the Seleucid era began in the fall, the 1st year having its beginning Dios 1 (October 7), 312 B.C. However, in the Babylonian calendar the years of the Seleucid era had their beginning in the spring, the first year having started Nisanu 1 (April 3), 311 B.C.[22] But these earlier eras were only forerunners of the Christian era, which is the basis for the modern dating that has spread over much of the globe. It is important to this study, because from its starting point modern historians reckon not only subsequent events but also, in the other direction, all past history in the B.C. dating scale. It is in terms of B.C. years that the regnal years of Artaxerxes and other Biblical date formulas are made understandable.

The Christian Era

In the earlier centuries of the Christian church much dissension was caused by the various attempts to

---

[22] Parker and Dubberstein, *Babylonian Chronology* (1956), p. 20.

work out a satisfactory method of calculating the date of Easter. In the year now called A.D. 525, a monk named Dionysius Exiguus made a new 95-year Easter table. He copied the last years of the current table, soon to expire, which were numbered in the era of Diocletian; then, unwilling to preserve the memory of that persecuting emperor, he labeled the first column of his continuing, table "Anni Domini Nostri Jesu Christi" and numbered the first year 532.[23] From this came the present dating "in the year of our Lord" 532, and so on (Latin, *Anno Domini*, abbreviated to A.D.). Dionysius did not explain "532," but he evidently computed it from a date for Christ's birth that was already current in a 4th-century consular list.[24]

The English historian Bede (A.D. 673-735) adopted this dating in his improved Easter tables, which became the standard basis for dating purposes in annals and histories; then the Frankish rulers and later the popes began to date official documents in the new era, but it came only gradually into common use.[25] Al-

---

[23] Dionysius Exiguus, *Liber de Paschale*, in *Dionysii Exiguii [et al.]* . . . *Opera Omnia* ("Patrologia Latina," ed. J.-P. Migne, vol. 67), cols. 493-496; see also Charles W. Jones, "Development of the Latin Ecclesiastical Calendar," in his edition of *Bedae Opera de Temporibus*, pp. 68, 69.

[24] The birth of Christ is noted in a consular list in the *Chronographus Anni CCCLIIII* (in *Chronica Minora Saec. IV. V. VI. VII.*, vol. 1, p. 56) as occurring in the consulship of C. Julius Caesar Vipsanius and Lucius Aemilius Paulus, or A.U.C. 754. (This consular year is A.D. 1.)

W. H. P. Hatch (*An Album of Dated Syriac Manuscripts*, introduction, p. 19) says that Dionysius popularized a method already known; that dating from a supposed year of Christ's birth was introduced by Hippolytus of Rome (3d century), followed by Cyril of Scythopolis (6th century) and others. (For this Hatch cites R. P. Blake, "Po povodu daty armyanskago perevoda 'Tserkovnoǐ Istorii,' Sokrata Skholastica," in *Krĭstianskiǐ Vostok*, 5, pp. 175 ff., a Russian article on the Armenian version of the *Ecclesiastical History* of the 5th-century church historian Socrates Scholasticus.)

[25] Charles W. Jones, *op. cit.*, p. 70; see also Reginald L. Poole, *Medieval Reckonings of Time*, p. 40.

though Dionysius' dating of the birth of Christ was early recognized as erroneous, not all scholars to this day are agreed on what the correction should be.

As the Christian era was applied to historical dates, it was necessary to extend the scale of years backward. Events that had occurred in pre-Christian times were numbered as so many years before Christ's birth (abbreviated to B.C.). So the year preceding A.D. 1 was called 1 B.C., with no zero year between. As a consequence of this procedure, modern computation of ancient dates faces two inconveniences: (1) the year numbering before Christ runs in reverse, from larger to smaller figures, and (2) computations of intervals from B.C. to A.D. dates are hindered by the lack of a year 0; for example, a four-year lease made in 3 B.C. does not expire in A.D. 1, as would seem logical, but in A.D. 2. Astronomers have avoided this obstacle to computation by exchanging for the B.C. and A.D. notation a scale of negative and positive numbers, as on a thermometer, calling the year preceding A.D. 1 the year 0, and the year preceding that, *minus 1*.[26] Thus 1 B.C. is the same as the astronomical year 0, 2 B.C. is — 1, 3 B.C. is — 2, et cetera, the *minus* number being always *one less* than the corresponding B.C. number. It is also to be noted that the leap years, which in our era are those divisible by 4, are not the same in B.C., but are 1, 5, 9, et cetera.

The following diagram illustrates the astronomical

---

[26] George F. Chambers, *A Handbook of Descriptive and Practical Astronomy,* vol. 2, p. 460.

and chronological reckoning, with the leap years marked by asterisks:

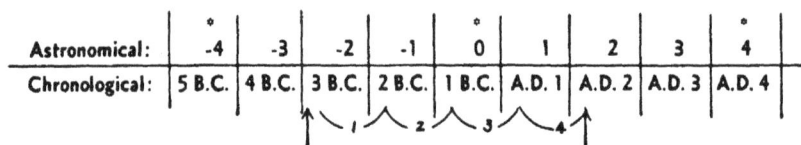

Astronomical:	-4	-3	-2	-1	0	1	2	3	4
Chronological:	5 B.C.	4 B.C.	3 B.C.	2 B.C.	1 B.C.	A.D. 1	A.D. 2	A.D. 3	A.D. 4

The fact that the year − 1 is 2 B.C., et cetera, has sometimes led to confusion. For example, many writers on the prophecies have computed the 70 weeks and the 2300 days (Dan. 9:24; 8:14) by straight subtraction thus: total number of years minus B.C. starting date equals A.D. ending date; but by doing this they inadvertently shorten the periods to 489 and 2299 years, respectively, instead of 490 and 2300.

The underlying principle can be illustrated by the imaginary four-year lease (see arrows on the preceding diagram) beginning some time in the year 3 B.C. (the astronomers' year − 2). If one attempts to compute the date of the expiration of the lease by subtracting 3 B.C. from the total of the four years, the result is A.D. 1 (4 − 3 = 1). But A.D. 1 is a year too early; a glance at the diagram shows that the four-year period would expire on the appropriate date in A.D. 2. The diagram thus demonstrates that simple subtraction of the B.C. date does not lead to the correct A.D. date. But the diagram reveals the fact that computation is simplified when the B.C. date is converted into its astronomical equivalent, − 2; then − 2 + 4 = 2 (or 4 − 2 = 2, which is the same thing) and the result is A.D. 2. Subtracting the *astronomical equivalent* [27] of the B.C. date from the total number of years always yields the correct A.D. terminal date.

Many 19th-century writers on the prophecies began the 70 weeks and the 2300 years from the 7th year of Artaxerxes, and most of these calculated the periods as extending from 457 B.C. to A.D. 33 and 1843 respectively, overlooking the fact that they were one year short; only a very few avoided error on the B.C.-A.D. transition, and arrived at A.D. 34 and 1844 respectively.[28] Generally those who made the error derived their dates from Ussher's chronology as given in margins of the Bible, or from subtraction: $490 - 457 = 33$, or $490 - 33 = 457$. Some of them cited the 18th-century astronomer James Ferguson for 457 B.C. and A.D. 33, not knowing that his "457 before Christ," written without a minus sign, was what astronomers now call -457, which is, according to the chronological system, 458 B.C. That Ferguson's dates were tabulated not in B.C. but in astronomical numbering is shown conclusively by his

---

[27] Those who prefer this stated algebraically will notice that, since the astronomical equivalent of a B.C. date is a negative number, it is not strictly correct to say that the negative number is to be subtracted; algebraically it is added, since adding a negative number is the same as subtracting a positive number.

[28] For a tabulation of these prophetic expositors, see L. E. Froom, *The Prophetic Faith of Our Fathers*, vol. 3, p. 744. Even William Hales, writing a work on chronology, explained the B.C. to A.D. transition and then, later in the same work, tripped over the zero year, and computed the 490 years by subtraction from 420 B.C. to A.D. 70. See his *New Analysis of Chronology*, 2d ed., vol. 1, p. 57; vol. 2, pp. 517, 518. The Millerites also made this mistake in the beginning, but later corrected their dates from A.D. 33 to 34 and from A.D. 1843 to 1844. For the basis of William Miller's computation see his *Evidence* (1836 ed.), pp. 49, 52; see further his manuscript "New Year Address" of 1844 reproduced in F. D. Nichol, *The Midnight Cry*, p. 172n and facsimile on p. 171. For the correction see the editorial "Chronology" in *Signs of the Times* 5 (1843), p. 123; A. Hale, "Diagram," and correction, *The Advent Herald*, 7 (1944), pp. 23, 77; S. S. Snow, "Prophetic Time," *ibid.*, p. 69.

use of the zero year, to which he was accustomed in his astronomical computations.[29] But this use of the zero year and negative numbers is rarely encountered by any except astronomers. Historical works give dates in the ordinary B.C. scale that has no zero year. Fortunately the need of such a zero year is ordinarily not felt except in computing an interval from a B.C. to an A.D. date.

After this survey of the various methods of counting years, two of which—the regnal-year systems and the B.C.-A.D. scale—are vitally important for a correct dating of Ezra 7, the next step is to consider the types of ancient calendars that have a bearing on the problem.

---

[29] Ferguson dealt with the 70 weeks as ending with the crucifixion, which he fixed by lunar calculation, according to the traditional Jewish calendar, at A.D. 33. See his *Astronomical Lecture, on . . . the True Year of Our Saviour's Crucifixion, . . . and the Prophet Daniel's Seventy Weeks;* for the zero year see "A Table of Remarkable Eras and Events," in his *Astronomy Explained Upon Sir Isaac Newton's Principles,* following sec. 396. The same table in his *Tables and Tracts, Relative to Several Arts and Sciences,* pp. 176-179, is followed by this sentence: "In this Table, the years both before and since CHRIST are reckoned exclusive from the year of his birth."

The fact that Ferguson's 457 is the ordinary 458 B.C. is shown also by other dates in the table (such as 775 instead of 776 for the beginning of the Olympiads, 746 instead of 747 for the era of Nabonassar, et cetera), and by the Julian period dates in his first column.

The Julian period (not to be confused with the Julian year) is an artificial scale proposed by Joseph J. Scaliger (about 1582) to avoid reckoning B.C. and A.D. dates in two directions. This period (abbreviated J.P.) was often used by older chronologists. It combines solar, lunar, and indiction cycles (28 × 19 × 15=7980 Julian years), beginning with a hypothetical 4713 B.C., when the first year of these several cycles would have coincided. The years J.P. 4713 and J.P. 4714 are exactly equivalent to 1 B.C. and A.D. 1 respectively. (Joseph J. Scaliger, *Opus de Emendatione Temporum,* rev. ed., book 5, pp. 359-361; *cf.* book 6, p. 600; see "Julian Period," in *Haydn's Dictionary of Dates;* also *The American Ephemeris* always gives the Julian period number for the current year, as J.P. 6682 for A.D. 1969.)

CHAPTER TWO

Ancient Civil Calendars

IN INTERPRETING ancient time statements we must deal not only with
systems of numbering years but also with various
calendars. Differing types of calendars are involved in
the time statements found in the Bible, and in historical
sources bearing on Bible chronology. Several of these
calendars will therefore be discussed next.

Calendars Based on Celestial Motions

Since calendars have been based on movements of
the earth, the moon, and the sun, an acquaintance with
these movements is indispensable for an understanding
of the different ancient and modern calendars.

The day.—A natural unit of which every calendar
is composed is the day, a period of 24 hours, determined
by a rotation of the earth on its axis. Since the sunrise
and the sunset mark two clearly recognizable points of
time in that 24-hour period, people have never had any
difficulty in designating the day, whether they began it
at sunset, as for instance the Babylonians [1] and Israelites [2]
did, or at dawn, as was done among the Egyptians. [3] The

---

[1] Parker and Dubberstein, *Babylonian Chronology* (1956), pp. 1, 26.
[2] Gen. 1:5, 8, etc.; Lev. 23:32; *cf.* Mark 1:32.
[3] Richard A. Parker, *The Calendars of Ancient Egypt*, p. 10. Ptolemy's computations seem to indicate that in his time the day began at sunrise.

beginning of the day at midnight is a comparatively late invention, which was not introduced before Roman times.[4]

The month.—The next larger calendar unit recognizable by an observation of natural phenomena is the month, which approximately coincides with one revolution of the moon around the earth. Since this revolution is accomplished in 29.53059 days, the various months cannot be of equal length as expressed in terms of whole days, which is a natural procedure. Therefore lunar months, as they were used by many ancient peoples and some modern nations, have an alternating length of 29 and 30 days.

The beginning of the lunar month is difficult to determine by observation, because the moon is ordinarily invisible to the human eye at the time of conjunction, usually called new moon in calendars and almanacs. The moon is at conjunction at the moment when, on her revolution around our globe, she stands between the sun and the earth, so that the half of that celestial body turned toward us receives no light from the sun and lies therefore in complete darkness. Sometimes when the moon stands exactly between the earth and the sun her shadow strikes the earth, causing in this way a partial or total eclipse of the sun during

---

[4] Pliny *Natural History* ii. 79 (Loeb ed., vol. 1, pp. 319, 321); Varro, cited in Aulus Gellius *Attic Nights* iii. 2 (Loeb ed., vol. 1, pp. 239, 241); Plutarch *Moralia*, "The Roman Questions," no. 84 (Loeb. ed., vol. 4, pp. 129, 131); Censorinus *De Die Natale* 12 [23] (Maude trans., pp. 36, 37). The statements of these classical authors are correct with regard to the beginning of the day among the Romans, but a word of caution is in place concerning their remarks, mostly erroneous, about the beginning of the day among other peoples.

the short period of conjunction. These are the only times when the conjunction of the moon can actually be observed.

In the Near East it takes 16.5 to 42 hours after conjunction [5]—depending on whether her movements in relation to her distance from the earth are fast or slow—before the moon becomes visible again in the form of a thin crescent, waxing larger and larger until the time of the full moon. The full moon is said to be in opposition, since the sun and the moon stand opposite each other as seen by an observer on this earth. After full moon the visible shape of that body wanes until it becomes invisible from about 42 to 16 hours before the conjunction, by which time one "astronomical lunar month" has been completed.

Since the conjunction of the moon is invisible, the ancients who used a lunar calendar depended either on the first visibility of the new crescent to determine the beginning of each new month, as did the Babylonians,[6] or on the disappearing of the old moon before conjunction, as the Egyptians.[7] The interval between the conjunction of the moon and the evening on which the first crescent can be observed has not yet received a universally recognized term; it will be called in this study the "translation period."

The year.—The largest calendrical unit, the year, is measured by one revolution of the earth around the

---

[5] Parker, *The Calendars of Ancient Egypt*, p. 4.
[6] Parker and Dubberstein, *Babylonian Chronology* (1956), p. 1.
[7] Parker, *The Calendars of Ancient Egypt*, pp. 9-23.

sun, which averages 365.2422 days, or about 12⅓ lunar months. This natural solar (or tropical) year, marked off by the recurrence of easily observable seasons, has four cardinal points: the summer and winter solstices, when the sun's apparent path in the sky lies farthest north and south, respectively; and the vernal and autumnal equinoxes, when the sun rises and sets in the exact east and west, with equal day and night over the whole globe. But the solar year is not exactly divisible by lunar months or even by whole days, a circumstance that has given rise to a number of different schemes to harmonize a calendar year, reckoned in whole days, with the astronomical year.

Solar calendar.—Of the several systems of reckoning solar years that have been in use in ancient times, the Egyptian and Julian calendar years were the most important. The ancient Egyptians, using the solar year for chronological purposes, had 12 equal months of 30 days each and, in addition, 5 extra days, which were appended to the end of the 12 months, giving to the whole year 365 days. This calendar, however, was still about ¼ of a day shorter than the astronomical year, a whole day every 4 years, or 10 days every 40 years. The ancient Egyptians never took measures to correct this situation; consequently their calendar slipped backward through all the seasons of the year in the course of 1,460 years, as will be explained later.[8]

The Julian calendar (likewise explained later), which was introduced by Julius Caesar, corrected the

---

[8] See the next section on the Egyptian calendar, pp. 36-43.

ANCIENT CIVIL CALENDARS

deficiency of the Egyptian solar calendar by making every fourth year consist of 366 days, instead of the 365 days of the common year. But even this reform of the calendar was not sufficient, since the year is somewhat short of 365¼ days. In the time of Pope Gregory XIII (A.D. 1572-1585) the Julian calendar had slipped far enough out of line with the seasons to call for a further correction. Today most Western nations use the Gregorian calendar, which is a very slightly modified Julian calendar.[9]

Luni-solar calendar.—Because of their annual festivals, which must come always in the same seasons, the ancient Assyrians, Babylonians, and Hebrews, like most ancient nations that used lunar calendars, had to insert extra months periodically to keep the lunar year in harmony with the solar year, which is about 11 days longer.

The early Assyrians had only 12 lunar months, but they observed that after every 2 or 3 years the end of the 12th month did not quite reach the season in which the New Year's Day should fall. Then they shifted their New Year's Day one lunar month later. In this way the beginning of their year would fall, in the course of time, in every one of their 12 lunar months. In the 12th century B.C. they accepted the principal features of the Babylonian calendar, which followed a slightly different system.[10]

---

[9] See pp. 43-45 for the Julian and Gregorian calendars.

[10] Ernst F. Weidner, "Der altassyrische Kalender," *Archiv für Orientforschung,* 5 (1928-29), pp. 184, 185; also his "Aus den Tagen eines assyrischen Schattenkönigs," *Archiv für Orientforschung,* 10 (1935-36), pp. 27-29.

The Babylonian lunar calendar made the same adjustment to the solar year by counting either the 6th or the 12th month twice in every 2d or 3d year; thus the New Year's Day always fell on the first day of the first month, *Nisanu,* and in nearly the same location in the solar year.[11] This calendar was adopted, as already mentioned, by the Assyrians in the 12th century B.C. The Jews had a similar calendar, as will be explained in the next chapter.

After these preliminary explanations, a discussion of the several calendars with which this study is concerned must be undertaken.

The Egyptian Calendar

The Egyptians used several different calendars throughout their ancient history, but for this study only the civil calendar, based on the solar year, is of importance. The Egyptian lunar calendar, used only for festival purposes, can be disregarded here.

The solar year.—It is not quite certain how the Egyptians came to the conclusion that the year consisted of exactly 365 days, but O. Neugebauer has advanced the theory that they arrived at it gradually as they learned that the annual inundation of the Nile happened at an average interval of 365 days.[12] Since we know that the Egyptians kept careful records of the

---

[11] Parker and Dubberstein, *Babylonian Chronology* (1956), p. 1.

[12] O. Neugebauer, "Die Bedeutungslosigkeit der Sothisperiode für die älteste ägyptische Chronologie," *Acta Orientalia,* 17 (1938), pp. 169-195; also his "The Origin of the Egyptian Calendar," *Journal of Near Eastern Studies* (hereinafter abbreviated to *JNES*), 1 (1942), pp. 396-403.

annual inundations from very early times, it is possible that their 365-day solar year was developed in this way.

Previously the most widely accepted theory was that of Eduard Meyer, maintaining that astronomical observations lay at the basis of the Egyptian solar year.[13] From very early times the annual feast of Sothis was celebrated on the day of the heliacal rising of the star Sothis, which we call Sirius, that is, on the day when the star first rises in the eastern sky shortly before sunrise, after a period during which it has been too close to the sun for visibility. The day of this first morning rising of Sirius, which during the dynastic period of Egypt ranged from July 17 to 19,[14] was for many centuries celebrated as a feast day. It has been thought that the observation of Sirius' heliacal rising was the origin of the 365-day solar year.

To this should be added the fact that the first of the three seasons into which the Egyptian year is divided is called 'Akhet, meaning "inundation." The inundation by the Nile starts in early June in Egypt, and the beginning of the year seems, therefore, to have been at a time of the Sothis feast. When the Egyptians had discovered that the heliacal rising of Sothis occurred approximately every 365 days, harmonizing with the beginning of the Nile inundation, the year of 365 days was a logical development.

---

[13] Eduard Meyer, "Aegyptische Chronologie," *Abhandlungen der Königlichen Preussischen Akademie der Wissenschaften*, Berlin, 1904, Phil.-Hist. Klasse, part 1, pp. 1-212; also his "Nachträge zur ägyptischen Chronologie," *ibid.*, 1907, part 3, pp. 1-46.
[14] Parker, *The Calendars of Ancient Egypt*, p. 7.

After the year had thus been fixed, their conservatism prevented any change, even though they observed that every four years the heliacal rising of Sirius came one day later in their calendar, or, to express it another way, the Egyptian New Year's Day fell one day earlier than the Sothis Day, since a year of 365 days is approximately ¼ of a day shorter than the actual solar year. Thus every four years the failure to add an extra day made all Egyptian dates slip back one day earlier in relation to the seasons, until finally New Year's Day would make the complete circuit of the seasons and again coincide with the heliacal rising of Sothis 1,460 years later.[15]

In a lifetime the seasonal shift was not very great, amounting to only 15 days in 60 years. A keen observer, however, might have been able to tell as an old man that the inundation started 2 weeks later in the Egyptian calendar than when he was a child, 60 years before.

The Egyptian year was divided into three seasons of four months each: (1) *'Akhet* "inundation," (2) *Peret,* meaning "emergence" of the fields from the water, and (3) *Shemu* "summer." [16] It is assumed that these names were given to the three sections of the calendar year when they synchronized with the actual seasons as they occurred in Egypt. However, the three calendrical seasons moved back one day every four years with the "wandering" Egyptian year. Thus after 120 years the season which was called "inundation"

---

[15] Alan H. Gardiner, *Egyptian Grammar,* pp. 203-205.
[16] *Ibid.*

38

would precede the actual inundation by the Nile by 30 days, and after 360 years, it would precede it by 3 full months. This apparently did not disturb the Egyptians any more than we are disturbed by our habit of designating October 15, 1969, by the formula 10/15/69, although we know that October means literally the "eighth" month, not the tenth.

The Egyptian calendar has been called a "wandering calendar" because every date, by shifting back one day every four years, "wandered" through all the seasons of the astronomical year in the course of 1,460 years, and this cycle of 1,460 years is called a "Sothic cycle," since New Year's Day returns to the date of the heliacal rising of Sothis, or Sirius, in that number of years.

In the earlier periods of Egyptian history there were no names for the months of the civil year, and the formula "In the 3d month of *Peret*" can be translated as meaning in the 7th month of the year. At the end of the three seasons of four 30-day months each, which totaled 360 days, 5 extra days, the so-called "epagomenae," were added to complete the 365-day year.

From the middle of the second millennium B.C. the months came gradually to be designated no longer by numerals but by names that had been in use in the lunar calendar. In the later period, with which our study is concerned, these month names were used exclusively. Since they are used in the dates of the Aramaic papyri to be studied below, they are therefore listed herewith:

Thoth	30 days	Pharmuthi	30 days
Phaophi	30 "	Pachons	30 "
Athyr	30 "	Payni	30 "
Choiak	30 "	Epiphi	30 "
Tybi	30 "	Mesore	30 "
Mechir	30 "	Epagomenae	5 "
Phamenoth	30 "		
		Total	365 days

The regularity and simplicity of the Egyptian calendar, as one can see from the list given,[17] make it easy to convert an Egyptian date into its equivalent in the Julian calendar for the periods in which the New Year's Day is known. This has been made possible for the 7½ centuries preceding the birth of Christ by the Greek-Egyptian astronomer, Ptolemy, whose work needs some consideration here.

Ptolemy's Canon.—Claudius Ptolemaeus, or Ptolemy, was a noted mathematician, astronomer, and geographer who lived at Alexandria in the second century of our era. He is most famous for his astronomical theory, embodied in a monumental Greek work on astronomy entitled *Mathematike Syntaxis* ("Mathematical Composition"), but better known by the Arabic name *Almagest*. This work, which survives in its entirety, is an embodiment and elaboration of the work of Hipparchus of Rhodes, whose writings are not extant. The Ptolemaic theory, envisioning the earth as a globe around which the heavenly bodies revolve in a

---

[17] Parker, *The Calendars of Ancient Egypt*, p. 8.

complicated system of circles, formed the standard explanation of the universe for 1400 years.[18]

In the *Almagest*, Ptolemy frequently gives observational data to demonstrate his theories of the motions of the moon and other heavenly bodies. In this work he mentions 19 lunar eclipses ranging over 9 centuries, dated to the year, month, day, and hour, mostly in terms of regnal years of various kings.[19] These are extremely valuable for chronology, because they enable the modern astronomer to check on Ptolemy's calculations. Since the intervals between these observations were important to Ptolemy's theory of celestial motions, he gave as a sort of appendix to the *Almagest* a list, or canon, of kings, with the length of each reign, to serve as a chronological scale for his astronomical data.[20]

The first king listed in Ptolemy's Canon is the Babylonian monarch Nabonassar, whose first regnal year began according to Egyptian reckoning on Thoth 1, the Egyptian New Year's Day, on the Julian date that has been established by lunar eclipses as February 26, 747 B.C.[21] This is the starting point of what is called

---

[18] Henry Norris Russell, Raymond Smith Dugan, John Quincy Stewart, *Astronomy*, vol. 1, pp. 243, 244; Agnes Mary Clerke, "Astronomy: History of Astronomy," *Encyclopaedia Britannica*, vol. 2 (1945), p. 583.

[19] Ptolemy *Almagest* iv. 6-9, 11, and v. 14, etc. Trans. R. Catesby Taliaferro, in "Great Books of the Western World," vol. 16, pp. 123, 129, 134-137, 140-142, and 172, etc.

[20] See Appendix 1, p. 128, in the present work.

[21] This date can be established because Ptolemy not only dates the eclipses to the hour in his own calendar reckoning but also gives in most cases the number of Egyptian (365-day) years, days, and hours from the starting point of the era. (See Ptolemy, *op. cit.*, pp. 140-142, 172, for example.)

As to the possibility of confusing any of these eclipses with others occurring on the same date of different years, it is to be noted that a lunar eclipse comes only at full moon. A full moon can occur on the same date in our calendar only

41

the Nabonassar era. The canon gives the number of regnal years of each king listed—first the Babylonian rulers, followed by the Persians, Alexander the Great and his Ptolemaic successors in Egypt, and finally the Roman emperors, ending with Antoninus Pius. Ptolemy's intention was not to give a complete historical list of reigns, but rather to have a convenient chronological scale to establish the intervals between his various astronomical observations discussed in the *Almagest.* So long as every year in the scale carried a regnal number, it served Ptolemy no useful purpose to list kings who reigned less than a year; hence it is not surprising that these are not included.

Regardless of the various modes of reckoning employed in the countries involved, Ptolemy consistently used his own Egyptian calendar with its 365-day year. Since the starting point of his Nabonassar era on Thoth 1 of the year 747 B.C. (February 26) is established by 19 lunar eclipses, we can locate any year of any of these kings as *reckoned by the Egyptian calendar year,* and

---

every 19 years, but can recur in the Egyptian calendar, which shifts backward through the seasons, only about every 25 years (see pp. 131-132). For a graphic representation of this recurrence in the Julian and Egyptian calendars, see Lynn H. Wood, "The Kahun Papyrus and the Date of the Twelfth Dynasty (With a Chart)," *Bulletin of the American Schools of Oriental Research* (hereinafter abbreviated to *BASOR*), no. 99 (October, 1945), pp. 5-9. Besides, not all full moons can be eclipsed; this can take place only about twice a year. Therefore the possibility of a lunar eclipse recurring on the same Egyptian date is reduced still more.

Further, Ptolemy's 19 eclipses, dated by year, day, and even hour, are all in mutual agreement, and various astronomers who have calculated these eclipses by modern methods have all agreed on their dates, varying only slightly as to the hour. Oppolzer's tables of lunar eclipses show that the average variance between his computations and Ptolemy's statements is about ten minutes. (For the lunar eclipses of Ptolemy, see Theodor von Oppolzer, *Syzygien-Tafeln für den Mond,* pp. 31-34; for the astronomical data, see his *Canon der Finsternisse,* pp. 332 ff.)

can compute it in B.C. dating. This is an easy process, because the Egyptian New Year's Day drops back one day every four years in the Julian calendar, which is used for B.C. reckoning.

The Julian Calendar

The Julian calendar, named after Julius Caesar, who introduced it into the Roman world, formed the next step in a logical development of the Egyptian solar calendar by adopting its 365-day year and approximately correcting its ¼-day drift.

The earlier Roman calendar used a lunar year. Since a lunar year is shorter than the natural solar year, it needs to be lengthened periodically, as has been explained, to keep the months in line with the seasons. In Caesar's time the Roman calendar had been allowed to drift more than two months out of alignment because the officials had failed to make the necessary additions from time to time. Finally Julius Caesar took drastic steps to remedy the situation. Correcting the backward displacement by a 445-day year, he introduced, on January 1, 45 B.C., a purely solar calendar, designed by the Egyptian astronomer Sosigenes. This was based on the Egyptian 365-day year, but it provided for the addition of a day every four years, an improvement the Egyptians had never made for themselves. Caesar retained the January 1 New Year's Day (the beginning of the consular term of office); and he kept the older month names as well—even the obsolete September, October, November, and December, which had once been months 7 through 10, as their names indicate.[22]

When Caesar's successor, Augustus, made Egypt a part of the Roman Empire, he introduced the Julian leap-year scheme into the original Egyptian calendar, pinning the formerly wandering Thoth 1 to August 29 (August 30 once in four years, in the summer preceding each Julian leap year). During the period of the empire various eastern provinces adjusted their old months to the Roman calendar. The Syriac version of the Julian calendar, for example, still survives in most Arab countries today alongside the uncorrected lunar calendar of the Moslems.[23] It preserves most of the old Semitic lunar month names, beginning therefore with *Teshrin I,* which coincides with our October and has 31 days, and its month *Shubat,* coinciding with our February, has 28 or 29 days.[24]

The Julian calendar was taken over, month names and all, in the western provinces. Consequently it was used in the European world universally until the Gregorian revision of 1582, and in many countries much later than that. In fact, the Gregorian calendar is the same as the Julian, except for the elimination of three leap-year days every four centuries.[25]

---

[22] F. E. Adcock, "Caesar's Dictatorship," *CAH*, vol. 9, p. 696; Dio Cassius *Roman History* xliii. 26 (Loeb ed., vol. 4, p. 259); Plutarch *Julius Caesar* 59 (Loeb ed., vol. 7, pp. 579, 581).

[23] The Moslem calendar has 12 lunar months, and does not have a system of inserting intercalary months as in the Babylonian and Jewish calendars. Therefore it runs about 11 days short every year, frequently making the circuit of the seasons.

[24] Ginzel, *Handbuch*, vol. 1, pp. 225-228, 263, 264; see also Parker, *The Calendars of Ancient Egypt*, p. 8; G. W. Thatcher, *Arabic Grammar*, p. 218.

[25] When Caesar adopted a 365-day year from Egypt, he eliminated the backward drift of the calendar (see pp. 34, 35, 38) by introducing leap years, of 366 days each, once every 4 years. However, the true solar year is a fraction *less* than

ANCIENT CIVIL CALENDARS

Astronomers employ the Julian reckoning unchanged to this day because of its convenient regularity, and historians date all pre-Christian events in the Julian scale extended backward theoretically, as if it had been in use throughout.

The Babylonian Calendar

The Babylonians celebrated their New Year's Day in the spring, which was the natural thing to do in the Mesopotamian Valley. As soon as the snows melt in the Armenian mountains, the volume of water in the two rivers, Tigris and Euphrates, increases so much that the canals of the irrigation system in lower Mesopotamia are filled, and cause new life to spring up every-

---

365¼ days. Hence adding one day *every* 4 years, or 100 in 4 centuries, results in a slight overcorrection, since only 97 leap years in 4 centuries are required to keep the calendar in step with the sun. Consequently, as long as the Julian calendar was in use, the equinoxes and solstices, which mark off the 4 seasons of the true year, completed their circuit a fraction earlier in relation to the calendar year, and thus eventually fell on earlier calendar dates.

This gradual change eventually caused concern because of its effect on the date of Easter, which came later and later in the spring. In the 4th Christian century, when the method of calculating Easter was first settled, the date of spring equinox was March 21. This calendar date had gradually moved forward so much that in 1582 it came 10 days after the equinox, the latter being March 11 in 1582.

Astronomers had long advocated correcting the displaced year. Hence Pope Gregory XIII undertook to restore March 21 as the date of the vernal equinox, and thus also Easter to the place it had held in the 4th century. He decreed that the day following Thursday, Oct. 4, 1582, should not be called Friday, Oct. 5, but Friday, Oct. 15, thus dropping out 10 day numbers from the calendar to correct for the 10 excess leap-year days that had been inserted since the beginning of the 4th century. Further, he ruled that the year should be reckoned uniformly from January 1. (See note 20 in chapter 4.) And to prevent new discrepancies between the calendar year and the astronomical year, he decreed that henceforth those century years that were not divisible by 400 (1700, 1800, 1900, 2100, etc.) were not to be counted as leap years.

This Gregorian calendar was immediately accepted by Catholic countries, but not by Protestant countries until much later. England and the American colonies introduced it only in 1752, by which time the counting of A.D. 1700 as a leap year had increased the error to 11 days. Eastern European countries have adopted it only in the present century. (Peter Archer, *The Christian Calendar and the Gregorian Reform*, pp. 10, 11, 75; John Gerard, "Chronology," *The Catholic Encyclopedia*, vol. 3, pp. 739, 740.)

45

where. The vernal equinox may also have had an influence on the establishment of the New Year's Day in the
spring, but this is not known. Whatever may have been
the reason, we know that in Babylonian history, from
earliest times, New Year's Day fell in March or April.[26]
The Babylonians did not have a pure solar year,
and their so-called luni-solar year consisted of 12
months of unequal length, having either 29 or 30 days
each, giving to a 12-month lunar year a total of 354 or
355 days. Since the lunar year was approximately 11
days shorter than the solar year, either the 6th month,
Ululu, or the 12th month, *Addaru,* was repeated every
2d or 3d year.[27] Such a 13-month year, called an embolismic (leap) year, had 383 or 384 days.

Earlier than the fourth century B.C. there was not
always a clear sequence in the insertion of embolismic
months, but when by observation it was recognized that
19 solar years contain approximately the same number
of days as 235 lunar months, a more regular sequence
of intercalation was started. In the 4th century, the
so-called 19-year cycle, in which the 3d, 6th, 8th, 11th,
14th, 17th, and 19th years were embolismic ones, became a regular feature of the luni-solar year in Mesopotamia. This regularity had already been achieved
more or less in the 6th century B.C., but exceptions
show some elasticity prior to the 4th century.[28]

---

[26] S. Langdon, *Babylonian Menologies and the Semitic Calendars,* pp. 1 ff.
[27] Parker and Dubberstein, *Babylonian Chronology* (1956), p. 1.
[28] *Ibid.,* pp. 2, 6. The pattern of embolismic years is known (commonly numbered as the 3d, 6th, 8th, etc., of each cycle), but this *numbering* is modern; there
is no known ancient record that specifically designates any given regnal year as
"year 1" of the Babylonian 19-year cycle.

In the early history of Babylon there seems to have been no regular system for determining when *Ululu* (the 6th month) or *Addaru* (the 12th month) should be repeated. Later on, when the 19-year cycle became more fixed, the second *Addaru* was inserted six times and the second *Ululu* once (in each 17th year) in each cycle. For this calendar the excellent monograph of R. A. Parker and W. H. Dubberstein, *Babylonian Chronology 626* B.C.-A.D. *75*, has complete calendar tables containing all embolismic years as known up to the time of publication, and approximately correct dates for the beginning of every Babylonian month for the time indicated in the title.[29] This work allows us to convert without effort any Babylonian date into its Julian equivalent with fairly great accuracy.

The Babylonian practice of beginning each month after the first visibility of the new crescent is responsible for the irregular length of the months. Since the beginning of their months was dependent upon the observers' eyesight and upon the weather, months were occasionally started a day later than they could have begun if the weather had been more favorable, and if the first crescent had been visible the evening before. Therefore, in one year *Nisanu* or any other month might have 29 days and in another year, 30. The reconstruction of the Babylonian calendar as done most recently, in the work of Parker and Dubberstein, bases its dates for the beginning of the months on an average

---

[29] *Ibid.*, pp. 27-47.

reasonable "translation period," but dates that are arrived at in this way may be off by one day, as the authors admit for their tables.[30] These facts give to the Babylonian calendar always a degree of uncertainty that is absent from the fixed solar calendar of the Egyptians. For all practical purposes, dates expressed in terms of the Babylonian calendar from the 8th century B.C. onward can generally be fixed with a margin of error of only one day. However, it must always be remembered that absolute certainty cannot be achieved in Babylonian dates.

The month names of the Babylonians,[31] which were taken over by the Jews during the exile, are the following (with the Jewish names in parentheses [32]):

1. Nisanu (Nisan)	8. Arahsamnu (March-
2. Aiaru (Iyyar)	eshvan or Heshvan)
3. Simanu (Sivan)	9. Kislimu (Kislev)
4. Duzu (Tammuz)	10. Tebetu (Tebeth)
5. Abu (Ab)	11. Shabatu (Shebat)
6. Ululu (Elul)	12. Addaru (Adar)
7. Tashritu (Tishri)	

After having covered the principal ancient calendars that will be encountered in the dates of the documents to be discussed, the next chapter will take up the study of the Hebrew calendar.

---

[30] *Ibid.*, p. 25.
[31] *Ibid.*, p. 26.
[32] Seven of the 12 Babylonian month names are mentioned in the postexilic books of Zechariah, Esther, Ezra, and Nehemiah, the references being the following: (1) Nisan, Esther 3:7; Neh. 2:1; (3) Sivan, Esther 8:9; (6) Elul, Neh. 6:15; (9) Chisleu (Kislev), Zech. 7:1; Neh. 1:1; (10) Tebeth, Esther 2:16; (11) Shebat, Zech. 1:7; (12) Adar, Esther 3:7, 13; 8:12; 9:1, 15, 17, 19, 21; Ezra 6:15.

CHAPTER THREE

The Pre-Exilic Hebrew Calendar

SINCE THE Jewish calendar of Ezra 7 is a continuation of that used before the Babylonian exile, a study of the Hebrew calendar as it can be reconstructed from the pre-exilic records must precede the discussion of the postexilic calendar system.

In this reconstruction we are on a more insecure foundation than in regard to the calendars of the Egyptians and Babylonians. The reason for this uncertainty is the poverty of source material. In Mesopotamia tens of thousands of cuneiform tablets give all the information necessary to reconstruct the Babylonian calendar so that a comparatively clear knowledge of it can be gained. Our understanding of the Egyptian calendar is equally complete, but for that of the ancient Hebrews the Bible is virtually our only source material before the fifth century B.C. Furthermore, statements bearing on the subject are very few and far between, and in some cases not entirely clear.

The Noachic Calendar

The earliest calendar for which there is some Biblical evidence may have been solar, according to the records of the Flood (Gen. 7:11, 24, and 8:4). The rain began on the 17th day of the 2d month, and the waters prevailed 150 days, after which time the ark rested upon Mount Ararat on the 17th day of the 7th month. Since there are thus exactly 5 months, totaling 150 days, lying between the 17th of the 2d month and the 17th of the 7th month, the conclusion can be drawn that every month consisted of 30 days; hence there could have been no 29-day months. This observation has led some scholars to believe that Noah's calendar was a solar one consisting of 12 months of 30 days each, with some intercalary days at the end of the 12th month, as in the Egyptian calendar.[1]

Others have thought that the evidence points to a lunar year. Their argument is the following: The Flood began on the 17th day of the 2d month in the 600th year of Noah (Gen. 7:11), and lasted until the 27th day of the 2d month in Noah's 601st year (ch. 8:13, 14), making a total of 1 year and 10 days. Since a lunar year is about 10 days shorter than a solar year, it is thought that the Flood therefore lasted one lunar year and 10 days, the length of one solar year. This latter view—that the entire period of the Flood was one solar year—is thought to be supported by the Septuagint translation of the Old Testament. Its translators, living in Egypt, where they were familiar with the Egyptian solar year, seem to reflect the tradition that the Flood

---

[1] For example, see several commentaries on Genesis 7 or 8, as *The Pulpit Commentary* citing Ewald, *The International Critical Commentary*, and Keil and Delitzsch.

lasted for one year, since they give its beginning as the 27th day of the 2d month instead of the 17th day.[2] Because of the poverty of evidence regarding this early period, it is impossible to say more about the calendar of Noah's time than to make these few remarks. But it should be pointed out that there is not the slightest evidence that either Noah or the Jews at any time had a calendar year of 360 days, which could be the basis of the *prophetic* year of that length.[3]

---

[2] This LXX date is one of a number of variations from the Hebrew text. They show a certain cons'stency and seem to have been based on the assumption that Noah's calendar year was solar. The data according to the LXX are the following:

(1) Beginning of the Flood	27th day, 2d month, 600th year
(2) Ark rests on Mt. Ararat	27th day, 7th month, ,, ,,
(3) Mountaintops visible	1st day, 11th month, ,, ,,
(4) Waters dried up	1st day, 1st month, 601st year
(5) Earth completely dry	27th day, 2d month, ,, ,,

The chief points are these: First, the duration of the Flood, between (1) and (5) is exactly one year. Second, the duration between the beginning of the Flood and its climax (1) and (2) is 150 days (chap. 7:24), and the two months' duration between (3) and (4) is explained in chap. 8:6-12 to have been 40 and 3 times 7 days, a total of 61 days. If, however, the Egyptian solar year was the basis of the dates given by the Alexandrian translators of the Flood record, they should have taken account of 5 epagomenal days inserted between the 12th and the first months, and their interval between (3) and (4) should have been 65 or (if both dates are included) 66 days instead of 61. This shows, as in so many other cases, that the variant readings of the LXX are by no means superior to those of the Hebrew text.

Several commentaries mention in connection with the Flood story the fact that 12 lunar months plus 10 days are approximately equivalent to a solar year. See, for example, Lange, *The Pulpit Commentary* (both of these citing Knobel); Kalisch; Skinner, in *The International Critical Commentary*. Medieval Jewish scholars differed on this point; Abraham Ibn Ezra says 1 solar year and 10 days, whereas Rashi says 1 lunar year and 10 days, totaling one solar year. See note on Genesis 8:14 in the *Soncino Books of the Bible*.

[3] The 3½ prophetic "times" of Daniel and the Revelation (Dan. 7:25; 12:7; Rev. 12:14) have been regarded from early times as 3½ years, generally reckoned as 360 days each, equivalent to the 1260 days (Rev. 11:3; 12:6) and to the 42 months (Rev. 11:2; 13:5) of 30 days each. Thus derived from prophetic periods, these are quite properly called *prophetic* years and months by many expositors. In the past, however, some authors, unfamiliar with the Jewish lunar calendar, have explained the 360-day year with 30-day months as an example of the official ancient Jewish usage.

Many of the leading expositors knew about the Jewish lunar year with its 29-day and 30-day months, or at least did not derive the 360-day prophetic reckoning from a calendar year at all, but from the obvious equivalence of the prophetic pe-

It is possible that the basis for the prophetic year of twelve 30-day months was the same as that of the Babylonian schematic calendar used for business purposes. This 360-day business year existed side by side with the real lunar-calendar year with its irregular sequence of 29- and 30-day months. Such a simplified calendar for business purposes proved to be useful for the past as well as for the future, since it eliminated the necessity of keeping exact records of the actual length of each month. The length of the months was ascertainable in regard to the past but not for the future until very late in the development of Babylonian astronomy. Therefore for many centuries contracts for future delivery were made up or rents and interest calculated (and even solstices or the reappearance of a star or planet predicted) according to a 360-day year and a 30-day month.[4] It was used merely as a uniform system of expressing future dates approximately.

riod of 3½ times with 1260 days (Rev. 12:6, 14) and of the 42 months with 1260 days (Rev. 11:2, 3). But other authors equally well known were misleading. G. S. Faber in 1806 calls the 360-day year "the old computation" (*A Dissertation on the Prophecies . . . of 1260 Years*, vol. 1, p. 4), and the following writers of the late 18th and early 19th centuries designate either the 30-day month or the 360-day year as Jewish reckoning: Thomas Newton, *Dissortations on the Prophecies*, dissertation 14. p. 192; Edward Bickersteth, *A Practical Guide to the Prophecies*, p. 135; George Croly, *The Apocalypse*, p. 161; William Cuninghame, *A Dissertation on the Seals and Trumpets . . . and the . . . Twelve Hundred and Sixty Years*, p. 115; Fessenden and Co.'s Encyclopedia of Religious Knowledge, art. "Month." The last-named work says that the Jews had a 365-day year like the Egyptians, with an intercalary month every 120 years!

The idea of a 365¼-day Jewish year reflects the opinion of earlier authorities, such as Scaliger (1583) and Funck (1570), from an age when knowledge of ancient chronology and calendation was still rudimentary. Ussher (1650) retains this view, but Prideaux (1719) dissents, holding that the Jews exchanged this type of year (which he attributes equally erroneously to the Chaldeans and Persians) for a lunar form with an intercalary month.

The confusion of a prophetic year with a nonexistent Jewish year illustrates the danger of following outmoded authorities.

[4] O. Neugebauer, "The Origin of the Egyptian Calendar," *JNES*, 1 (1942), pp. 400-401; see also his *The Exact Sciences in Antiquity*, p. 128.

THE PRE-EXILIC HEBREW CALENDAR

When the time came for fulfilling the contract, naturally an adjustment was made to the actual lunar-calendar date.

Even today theoretical months of 30 days each are used in computing interest, and it is possible that the practical Jews also had such an ideal business year, completely separated from the real calendar year. However, no evidence of the existence of such a year among the Jews has yet come to light, unless the prophetic 360-day year is taken as evidence for the existence of such a year.

Moses' Calendar Reform

The type of calendar in use by the Hebrews in Egypt before the Exodus is not known. It is possible that they used the Egyptian calendar with its wandering year or that they had preserved the Canaanite calendar, which seems to have been lunar, with its beginning in the fall. We know only from Exodus 12:2 that Moses received a divine command to fix the beginning of the year in the month in which the Exodus took place (*cf.* Num. 33:3), which is called *Abib* in chapter 13:4. *Abib* means "the month of ears," because the corn was then in the ear. This month (better known by its postexilic name of Nisan) fell for the most part in late March or April, since the barley harvest did not ordinarily begin before April in Palestine.

That the year in the Mosaic and post-Mosaic periods was lunar can be deduced from several Biblical statements. The Mosaic laws provided for offerings at

53

the time of the beginning of the "month" or "new moon," [5] giving special significance to this day (*cf.* Num. 28:11-14; 10:10). That the day of the new moon was the first day of the month in the time of Saul is evident from 1 Samuel 20:24, 27, where the day after the "new moon," when a royal banquet was held, was called "the second day of the month." So the Hebrew calendar from the time of Moses onward was undoubtedly lunar.

The Jews must have had a system of intercalation by which the lunar calendar was brought into harmony with the natural solar year. This is implied in the law dating the Passover feast unchangeably in the middle of the first month (Lev. 23:5) but also requiring the offering of a sheaf of the first fruits of grain (Lev. 23:10, 11). Thus the calendar was probably corrected by the insertion of embolismic months whenever needed to let the Passover occur at the beginning of barley harvest. This would automatically result in an average of seven embolismic months in nineteen years.

The Civil Year

The new ordinance fixing the beginning of the year in the spring implies that the Israelite year had hitherto begun at another time, probably in the fall. While from that time on the "ecclesiastical," or "sacred," year began in the spring, throughout the history of the Hebrew

---

[5] The word *chodesh*, derived from the root *chadash*, meaning "to renew," means in the first place "new moon," then "month." (See the edition of Gesenius' Hebrew dictionary by Brown, Driver, and Briggs.) *Chodesh* has the same meaning in Phoenician as in Hebrew. (See Zellig Harris, *A Grammar of the Phoenician Language*, p. 100.)

nation the existence of another type of year, called here "civil year," can be demonstrated from a number of Biblical and extra-Biblical evidences. This is also confirmed by the historian Josephus, who records the Jewish tradition on this point as existing in the first century of the Christian era. After speaking of an ancient reckoning beginning the year in the autumn, he continues:

"Moses, however, appointed Nisan, that is to say Xanthicus,[6] as the first month for the festivals, because it was in this month that he brought the Hebrews out of Egypt; he also reckoned this month as the commencement of the year for everything relating to divine worship, but for selling and buying and other ordinary affairs he preserved the ancient order."[7]

This civil fall-to-fall calendar probably synchronized with those in use among the pre-Israelite populations and was taken over either by the patriarchs or by the Jews after the conquest of Canaan.[8]

It has been observed that the Palestinian climate and seasons make an autumnal beginning the natural thing. This is the end of the dry and hot summer,

---

[6] Xanthicus is one of the Macedonian month names used rather widely in the eastern world during the Greek and Roman periods.

[7] Josephus *Antiquities* i. 3. 3 (Loeb ed., vol. 4, pp. 36-39).

[8] That the Hebrew civil calendar corresponded to the Canaanite calendar can first be shown by the fact that both began in the fall (Langdon, *op. cit.*, p. 24), and that three of the four pre-exilic month names mentioned in the Old Testament are attested in Phoenician inscriptions to be Canaanite.

Abib	1st month	(Ex. 13:4; 23:15; 34:18; Deut. 16:1).
Zif	2d month	(1 Kings 6:37).
Ethanim	7th month	(1 Kings 8:2).
Bul	8th month	(1 Kings 6:38).

For references to the Phoenician inscriptions mentioning the months Zif, Ethanim, and Bul, see Harris, *op. cit.*, pp. 84, 87, 98.

when everything has been dead and barren for several months. With the beginning of the early rain, new life springs forth, and it is natural to start the year from that point.[9]

A number of Hebrew expressions point to the fall-beginning year. The word *tequphah* is used in three Old Testament phrases indicating the end of a period of time. Derived from the hifil form of the verb *naqaph*, "to encircle" or "to make a circle," it means "turning point." The phrase *tequphôth hayyamim* (1 Samuel 1:20) means literally "at the rotation of days." The K.J.V. says "when the time was come about," applying it (as in the LXX, and followed by several commentators) to the number of days of Hannah's pregnancy. In Exodus 34:22 and 2 Chronicles 24:23 the phrase *tequphôth hashshanah* is correctly translated "at the year's end," and "at the end of the year," since the whole year had made one rotation and the new year was to begin. The parallel passage to Exodus 34:22 is found in chapter 23:16, where the word "end" is the rendering of the Hebrew word *se'th* (infinitive of *yaṣa'* in the construct state) meaning, "the going forth" or "the emergence." These texts, speaking of feasts that were to be celebrated in the 7th month of the ecclesiastical year, thus clearly state that they came after the end of the year, by which cannot have been meant the ecclesiastical year whose beginning fell in the spring. The texts quoted must there-

---

[9] Franz M. Th. Böhl, book review of Gustaf Dalman, *Arbeit und Sitte in Palästina*, vols. 1, 2, in *Archiv für Orientforschung*, 8 (1932-1933), p. 245.

fore refer to the beginning of the civil year, in the autumn.[10]

Another Hebrew term used in a chronological setting is *teshûbah*, meaning literally the "return." In 2 Samuel 11:1; 1 Kings 20:22, 26; 1 Chronicles 20:1; and 2 Chronicles 36:10 the phrase *teshûbath hashshanah* is used. In 1 Kings 20:22, 26 the K.J.V. translates the phrase in which this appears "at the return of the year." Its other three renderings, as in 2 Samuel 11:1, "after the year was expired," and the R.S.V. "in the spring," are really interpretations. In all these texts the Hebrew reads "return of the year." Although scholars are not unanimous in their interpretation of this word when it refers to the year,[11] the most plausible explanation is to consider it as an expression that indicates a turning point of the year halfway between the beginning and the end. The word *teshûbah* is derived from the Hebrew word *shûb*, which means "to turn" just as the English noun "return" originates from the verb "to turn." The author does not mean the beginning or the end of a certain period or journey, but its turning

---

[10] The word *tequphah* is explained by Brown, Driver, and Briggs as meaning "at the circuit (completion) of the year." Buhl's 17th edition of Gesenius explains it as "the rotation of the year, i.e. the autumnal or vernal equinoxes." Tregelles' edition of the same dictionary interprets it "after the course of a year." while Fuerst's Hebrew dictionary gives it as the "lapse of the year." The commentators have the same explanation, of which Curtis and Madsen's textual note in *The International Critical Commentary*, on 2 Chron. 24:23, may be given as an example, "at the coming round, circuit. i.e. at the completion of the year."

[11] The phrase *teshûbath hashshanah* is explained by Brown, Driver, and Briggs as "*the return of the year*, i.e. of spring," without calling it the end of the year. But several commentators have understood it so. Curtis and Madsen are non-committal in *The International Critical Commentary*, on 2 Chron. 36:10, but Lange says in his commentary on 1 Chron. 20:1, "When the year was ended, at the time when the kings go out, in the spring, as the most suitable for re-opening of the campaign," and on 1 Kings 20:22 the comment is made that it means "with the beginning of the next year."

point. The military campaigns, to which the texts refer, usually began in the spring, as we know from many ancient records. This shows that the spring was considered to be the turning point, lying halfway between the beginning and the end of the year, which points to the fall as the beginning of the civil year.

Solomon's Civil Calendar

From the time of Solomon we have another evidence for the fall-to-fall civil year. 1 Kings 6:1, 37, 38 states that the work on the Temple of Solomon began in the 2d month of the 4th year of the king and that it was completed in the 8th month of Solomon's 11th year, having been in building for 7 years.

If, in the Old Testament, months received numerals, they were always numbered from Abib, or Nisan, regardless of whether the reckoning of the year was from the spring or from the fall. In a year beginning with Ethanim (later Tishri), this 7th month in the ecclesiastical year was therefore *not* numbered as the 1st month of the civil year—although it was the first—but retained its number 7. A civil fall-to-fall year thus began with the 7th month, had the 12th month toward the middle, and ended with the 6th.[12] Hence, if two succes-

---

[12] It may seem strange at the first glance that the Jews should have labeled the first month of a certain calendar year the "seventh," but a similar practice is being followed today by many business firms that use fiscal years, which in most cases begin with our 7th month on July 1, and end June 30. Also the Jews of the present day are still using a calendar beginning with their 7th month, Tishri, as they have been doing for many centuries. Furthermore, the apparently contradictory custom of labeling the first month "seventh" finds its parallel in a similar procedure that has been followed since Roman times to the present day—that of designating the 9th month of the Julian or the Gregorian calendar by the name "September," which means literally "seventh month," the tenth month "October," which means "eighth month," etc.

sive events are dated in the 6th and the 7th months of one and the same regnal year of a king, it means that the year began with the 1st month as among the Babylonians, and that the 7th month followed the 6th in the same calendar year. If, however, two successive events are dated in the 9th and the 1st months of the same regnal year of a king—as for example in Nehemiah 1 and 2—the calendar is one in which the 1st month is not the beginning of a new year. See the two calendar schemes side by side in Table 1 on page 74.

Intervals beginning with an event are generally reckoned by anniversaries of that event and not, like the regnal years of the kings, by the calendar year.[13] Therefore, the 7 years of Temple building must be reckoned from the date of the beginning of building activities and not from the beginning of a calendar year.

In reckoning time periods the first and the last units of a period were usually included, whether they were complete or not. This method is called "inclusive reckoning." One out of many Biblical examples of the use of this method is found in 2 Chronicles 10:5, 12. Although Rehoboam had asked the people to return "after three days," "all the people came to Rehoboam on the third day, as the king bade." To us such a reckon-

---

[13] The example of Solomon's Temple building discussed here provides the strongest evidence for the correctness of this statement, since no other known system of computation leads to a harmonious solution of the data as given in the texts quoted. Other evidence for the existence of anniversary reckoning can be seen in the fact that certain feasts were memorial days or anniversaries of remarkable events, like the Passover held each year on the day when the Exodus had taken place (Ex. 13:3-8), or the Purim feast on the two days of the deliverance of the Jews from Haman's sinister plans of destruction (Esther 9:27).

ing would seem to be just as strange as if we should ask a man on Monday to return after three days and see him coming back on Wednesday instead of on Thursday as expected. For the ancient Hebrews "inclusive reckoning" was a commonly used method of computing time,[14] as also among other ancient peoples.[15]

If Solomon's regnal years began in the spring (with Nisan), and coincided with the ecclesiastical year, then the construction of the Temple would have occupied 8 years instead of 7, as Figure 2 shows. Only

The anniversary years of Temple building would number eight if Solomon's regnal years began in the spring (Nisan 1):

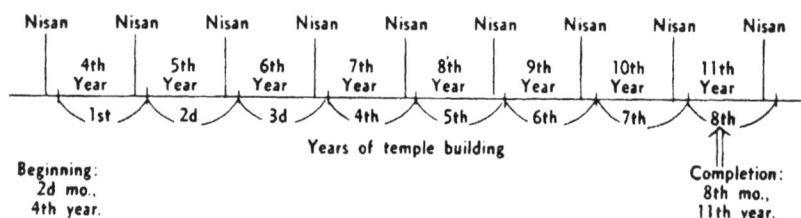

They would number seven if Solomon's regnal years began in the fall (Tishri 1):

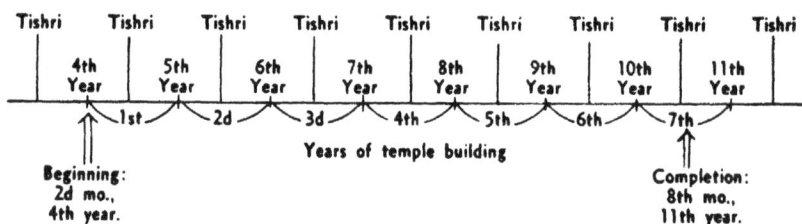

Fig. 2

---

[14] Other examples of Biblical inclusive reckoning: 2 Kings 18:9, 10; cf. Lev. 12:3 with Gen. 17:12; cf. Matt. 16:21 (also 17:23; 20:19) with Matt. 26:61; 27:63; and 12:40, in which the same author refers to the same interval as "the third day," "in three days," "after three days," and "three days and three nights" (see also texts in the other Gospels on this crucifixion-resurrection period). On inclusive reckoning see Thiele, op. cit., p. 28.

[15] For Greek and Roman examples, see H. J. Rose, "Calendar: Greek, Roman," Encyclopaedia Britannica (1945), vol. 4, pp. 578, 579; see definitions of English derivatives such as penteteric, octave, tertian fever, in an unabridged dictionary.

if we assume that his regnal years started in the fall (with Tishri) and that the 2d month in his 4th regnal year fell more than a half year after the civil New Year's Day, can we harmonize the different data given in the texts mentioned.[16]

The Gezer Calendar

From the same 10th century B.C., in which Solomon reigned, we have archeological evidence of the existence of a fall-to-fall calendar in Palestine. This comes to us in the form of a little limestone plaque found by Macalister during the excavations of the Palestinian city of Gezer.[17] Its text has been explained admirably by W. F. Albright[18] to cover the whole Palestinian calendar, and his translation is given here with a few additional remarks:[19]

"His two months are (olive) harvest;   (Sept.-Nov.)
his two months are grain-planting;   (Nov.-Jan.)
his two months are late planting;   (Jan.-March)
his month is hoeing up of flax;   (March-April)
his month is barley harvest;   (April-May)
his month is (wheat) harvest and
    festivity;   (May-June)
his two months are vine-tending;   (June-Aug.)
his month is summer-fruit."   (Aug.-Sept.)

---

[16] Thiele, *op. cit.*, pp. 28, 29.

[17] The latest and most thorough examination of the problems connected with the Gezer calendar was made by Albright, "The Gezer Calendar," *BASOR*, 92 (December, 1943), pp. 16-26. See also Albright's translation in J. B. Pritchard, ed., *Ancient Near Eastern Texts*, p. 320, for further pertinent bibliographical references.

[18] Albright follows scholars like Vincent, Macalister, Dalman, and others.

[19] Albright gives the translation on pp. 22, 23 of the *BASOR* article, with remarks as to which months are meant in notes 30, 32, 37, 38.

The Calendar of the Kingdom of Judah

The civil fall-to-fall calendar remained in use in the kingdom of Judah after Solomon's time throughout the 3½ centuries of its existence. This is shown by a careful analysis of all chronological data dealing with this period. The regnal years and the synchronisms contained in the books of Kings and Chronicles can be brought into a harmonious whole only by taking a fall-to-fall calendar as the basis of all civil reckoning in the kingdom of Judah.[20]

The existence of such a calendar during the time of King Josiah can be demonstrated without going into a lengthy discussion. 2 Kings 22:3 records that this king had repair work begun on the Temple in his 18th regnal year. We find, then, that his command was carried out, and funds were delivered to the workmen who did the repair job. During these activities the law book was found in the Temple. After it had been read before the king, and later in the presence of the elders, measures were taken to carry out the instructions found in that book. Josiah had all idolatrous places destroyed, first in Jerusalem and its surroundings, then in the remainder of his kingdom, from Geba to Beersheba, and

---

[20] Thiele, *op. cit.*, pp. 29-32. It might be mentioned here that a spring-to-spring civil calendar was apparently introduced in the kingdom of Israel by Jeroboam I when the ten tribes broke away from Judah. By assuming the existence of a calendar in Israel which differed from that of Judah, harmony can be reached between the various data provided in the books of Kings and Chronicles. (See Thiele, *op. cit.*, p. 30.) The practice of the northern kingdom, however, has no bearing on the main subject under discussion, the postexilic chronology of the Jews, who continued the practice of the southern kingdom of Judah. Therefore the mere acknowledgment of the existence of a variant calendar in Israel suffices.

finally extended his reformatory activities to the neighboring Assyrian province of Samaria. Having done all these things mentioned here briefly, the Passover was celebrated in his 18th year (2 Kings 23:23). The Passover was celebrated on the 14th day of the spring month (Lev. 23:5) later called Nisan, which was the first month of the ecclesiastical year. If Josiah had begun to reckon his 18th regnal year from Nisan, there would have been only two weeks between the beginning of the Temple repair and the celebration of the Passover to carry out all the different activities described in 2 Kings 22 and 23. Since everyone can see that it was absolutely impossible to do this in such a short time, it has to be assumed that his 18th regnal year began earlier than the 1st of Nisan, hence with the 1st of Tishri. This gave him more than 6 months' time to accomplish the different acts referred to before. That the statements found in 2 Kings 22 and 23 imply the existence of a fall-to-fall civil year has been recognized by scholars for a long time.[21]

Further evidence for the existence of a civil year beginning with the 7th month is provided by the story of the production of Jeremiah's scroll of prophecies as told in Jeremiah 36. Jeremiah was commanded to write the prophetic messages of his past ministry in a

---

[21] Thiele, *op. cit.*, pp. 29, 30. This Passover is cited as evidence for a pre-exilic Hebrew year beginning in the fall by Julius Wellhausen, *Prolegomena to the History of Israel*, trans. J. S. Black and Allan Menzies, p. 108. Many other scholars argue for a pre-exilic fall year; see W. O. E. Oesterley and Theodore H. Robinson, *A History of Israel*, vol. 2, p. 20; Adolphe Lods, *Israel From Its Beginnings to the Middle of the Eighth Century*, trans. S. H. Hooke, p. 436.

scroll *in the 4th year* of Jehoiakim (vs. 1, 2). After the scroll was written with the help of Baruch, his secretary, Baruch read it to the people of Jerusalem *in the 9th month of the 5th year* of Jehoiakim (v. 9). If a Nisan-to-Nisan calendar year had been in use among the Jews in Jeremiah's time, the composition of the scroll would have taken more than 8 months, even if begun at the end of the 4th year. This seems to be a much longer time than is warranted by the story. However, if the year began in the autumn with the 7th month (Tishri), the production of the scroll need not have taken much more than 2 months. It is certainly more likely that the scroll was produced in this shorter period of time.[22]

The use of this Tishri-to-Tishri calendar among the pre-exilic Jews is corroborated by a combination of extra-Biblical and Biblical evidence concerning the capture of Jerusalem by Nebuchadnezzar after the three months' reign of Jehoiachin of Judah. According to 2 Kings 24:12 this occurred in the 8th year of Nebuchadnezzar's reign, but the Babylonian Chronicle published in 1956[23] dates this event in Nebuchadnezzar's 7th year, on Adar 2 (approximately March 16, 597

---

[22] Julian Morgenstern used this argument as evidence for the existence of a royal year which, according to him, began at Tishri 1. See his "The New Year for Kings," in *Occident and Orient: Gaster Anniversary Volume*, pp. 442, 443.

[23] D. J. Wiseman, *Chronicles of Chaldaean Kings (626-556 B.C.) in the British Museum*, pp. 72, 73. This work is the most recently published portion (first printing 1956) of a series of segments of the annals of the Babylonian kings. The first, beginning with 747 B.C., was issued as *The Babylonian Chronicle* (1887), and other parts later under various titles (see Wiseman, *op. cit.*, pp. vi, 1-5). Since they all form parts of one historical narrative, the term Babylonian Chronicle is often used of the later portions as well as the one published under that title.

B.C.),[24] the earliest exact date for any Biblical event mentioned in secular records.

These divergent Biblical and Babylonian data for the same event need some explanation. In order to understand their value for our study, it is necessary to go back to Nebuchadnezzar's accession to the throne. The Babylonian Chronicle mentions that in the spring of the last regnal year of his father, Nabopolassar (605 B.C.), Nebuchadnezzar defeated the Egyptians in two battles—the first at Carchemish, the second at Hamath. After these victories he was pursuing the enemy toward their country when he received news that his father had died on Ab 8 (Aug. 15, 605). Thereupon he returned at once to Babylon and was crowned king on Elul 1 (Sept. 7, 605).[25] Since the Babylonians numbered the regnal years of their kings by the accession-year system, the period from Elul 1 to the end of the calendar year was considered Nebuchadnezzar's accession year, and his first regnal year began the next spring on Nisan 1, April 2, 604. Thus his 7th year, an embolismic year of 13 months, began March 27, 598, and ended April 12, 597. On Adar 2 of that 7th year Nebuchadnezzar captured Jerusalem and deposed the king (Jehoiachin), March 16, 597.

Let us now see how the Jewish annalists would date these events in their own autumn-to-autumn calendar.

---

[24] For convenience only one day number is given here and in subsequent Babylonian dates although, strictly speaking, the Babylonian day, beginning at sunset, covered parts of two days; thus more accurately, Adar 2 was March 15/16, sunset-to-sunset. *Cf.* Parker and Dubberstein, *Babylonian Chronology* (1956), p. 26.

[25] Wiseman, *op. cit.*, pp. 68, 69.

They also counted their own regnal years, and those of foreign kings as well, according to the accession-year system. On receiving news of Nabopolassar's death, which had occurred in the 5th month, they considered the remaining period of their calendar year as Nebuchadnezzar's accession year. However, their new year began with Tishri 1 (approximately Oct. 7, 605), the 1st day of the 7th month, and on that day the Jews began Nebuchadnezzar's 1st year, six months earlier than by Babylonian reckoning. Consequently, his 7th year, by Jewish reckoning, began approximately Oct. 1, 599, and ended Oct. 19, 598, six months before it ended in Babylonia. His 8th year began approximately Oct. 20, 598 and ended Oct. 8, 597. Therefore the capture of Jerusalem and of Jehoiachin, on March 16, 597, occurred in the 8th year of Nebuchadnezzar as the Jewish annalists recorded it.[26]

Therefore there is complete harmony between the seemingly conflicting "7th year" and "8th year" of the Babylonian and Biblical documents. The annalists of each country, using their own calendars, would have to date the same event in different regnal years of Nebuchadnezzar. This very fact is evidence that the Babylonians employed a spring-to-spring calendar and the Jews an autumn-to-autumn calendar, in which, respectively, they counted the regnal years of their own

---

[26] For a more detailed discussion of this period in Judah's history in the light of the Babylonian Chronicle see Horn, "The Babylonian Chronicle and the Ancient Calendar of the Kingdom of Judah," *Andrews University Seminary Studies* (hereafter abbreviated *AUSS*), 5 (1967), pp. 12-27. This article also presents the views of other scholars who have written on this subject and gives exhaustive bibliographical references in the footnotes.

kings, and of foreign kings as well.[27] If this simple explanation is accepted, there is no need for the rather strange assumption that the Jewish annalists antedated Nebuchadnezzar's reign but postdated their own kings,[28] or if not, that the Babylonian Chronicle records Jehoiachin's arrest and 2 Kings 24:12 his deportation later, after Nisan 1.[29]

The study of the pre-exilic records thus shows that aside from a possible solar calendar in Noah's time the Biblical calendar was lunar. It is also evident that Moses' introduction of a religious year beginning in the spring did not abolish an existing civil year which began in the fall, and that the regnal years of the kings of Judah were reckoned according to the civil fall-to-fall calendar from the time of Solomon to the end of the kingdom of Judah.

---

[27] It has already been pointed out that the astronomer Ptolemy followed the same custom by recording in his *Almagest* the regnal years of Babylonian, Persian, Greek, and other foreign rulers according to his own national calendar, namely that of Egypt. In the next chapter it will be shown that the Jewish colonists of Elephantine, Egypt, also followed this practice in the post-exilic period, by counting the years of Persian kings according to the local Egyptian calendar on the one hand and according to their own Jewish calendar on the other.

[28] Albright, "The Nebuchadnezzar and Neriglissar Chronicles," *BASOR*, no. 143 (October, 1956), p. 32; see D. N. Freedman, "The Babylonian Chronicle," *The Biblical Archaeologist*, 19 (1956), pp. 56, 57; Martin Noth, "Die Einnahme von Jerusalem in Jahre 597 v. Chr.," *Zeitschrift des Deutschen Palästina-Vereins*, 74 (1958), p. 155.

[29] Wiseman, *op. cit.*, p. 34; A. Malamat, "A New Record of Nebuchadrezzar's Palestinian Campaigns," *Israel Exploration Journal*, 6 (1956), p. 254. For another, equally improbable, theory see Thiele, *op. cit.*, pp. 167, 168.

CHAPTER FOUR

The Postexilic Jewish Calendar

THE KINGDOM of Judah ceased with the destruction of Jerusalem and the exile. Many time-honored institutions, like the fall-to-fall calendar, may temporarily have been given up, and it is conceivable, therefore, although not certain, that the Jews living in Mesopotamia adopted the Babylonian calendar. It is certain, however, that they adopted the Babylonian month names which from that time on were exclusively used in the Biblical and extra-Biblical Jewish literature.

After the Jews' return from exile it may have taken some time before innovations, like the adoption of the Babylonian calendar, were dropped once more in favor of old, venerated customs. It should therefore not be surprising to find some evidence for the existence of the Babylonian calendar either during or immediately after the Exile.

Ezekiel's Calendar

The chronological data presented in the book of Ezekiel are not sufficiently clear to arrive at final conclusions as to the type of calendar the exiled prophet used in Babylonia. His exilic era beginning with the captivity of Jehoiachin (Eze. 1:2) may have been reckoned by either (a) a spring-to-spring calendar, (b) one that counted the years by anniversaries from the day when the king had surrendered, approximately March 16, 597 B.C., or (c) a fall-to-fall calendar that began after the captives had arrived in Babylon in the fall of 597 B.C. Each one of the three systems would satisfy the different data given in this book in their relationship with those of Jeremiah and 2 Kings, as a careful study shows.[1]

The Calendar of Haggai and Zechariah

The prophet Haggai, giving his messages in the time of Zerubbabel, a few years after the completion of the Exile, is generally believed to have used the Babylonian spring-to-spring calendar. This has been deduced from the fact that in the records of Haggai the 6th month of the 2d year of Darius (chap. 1:1, 15) precedes

---

[1] A test case is Ezekiel 24:1, 2, in which the statement is made that Ezekiel had a vision on the very day when Jerusalem's siege began. The date given is the 10th day of the 10th month of the 9th year, by which the year of Jehoiachin's captivity must be meant according to Ezekiel 1:2 and 40:1. Through synchronisms between Biblical and Babylonian data—some of them astronomical—it can be shown that Jehoiakim's reign ended in December, 598 B.C. Jehoiachin, his son, was taken captive after a reign of only 3 months (2 Kings 24:8, 14-16). He was taken to Babylon by Nebuchadnezzar, who had begun his campaign, according to the Babylonian Chronicle, in the winter of 598/7 and had captured Jerusalem and its king March 16, 597 B.C. If Ezekiel began to count the years of his captivity according to the Babylonian calendar that began in the spring, his date for the foregoing vision would fall on the same day as the date given in 2 Kings 25:1 and Jeremiah 52:4 for the actual beginning of Jerusalem's siege. The same synchronism would result if the prophet dated the vision according to anniversary years, beginning the era of his captivity at some time between the spring and fall of 597 B.C., or if he began to reckon the years of the captivity after their arrival in the fall of 597 B.C. Only if the beginning of his era is extended back to the previous fall, when Jehoiakim was still on the throne, will a disagreement result between Ezekiel 24:1, 2 and 2 Kings 25:1.

the 7th and 9th months in the same 2d year of Darius (chap. 2:1, 10).[2]

For the type of Hebrew calendar used by Zechariah, Haggai's contemporary, the evidence contained in his book is not conclusive. Except for one date in Darius I's 4th year (chap. 7:1), only two dates are given for events that occurred in the ·same calendar year. Both months mentioned in these two dates—the 8th and the 11th months of Darius I's 2d year—fell between Tishri and Nisan (chap. 1:1, 7), so that it is not certain whether Zechariah used a calendar year beginning in the fall or in the spring. However, since he and Haggai worked together (Ezra 5:1), it is generally assumed that they followed one and the same calendar.

The Calendar of Esther

The chronological data of the book of Esther are not precise enough to reveal the nature of the Hebrew calendar, but leave the impression that the records

---

[2] The basis of this deduction is as follows: Haggai's first appeal to the leaders was made on the first day of the 6th month of Darius' 2d year (Haggai 1:1). The reason for the calamities that had struck the Jews was declared to have been their unwillingness to build the Temple while building their own homes. To the first speech was added an appeal to go to the mountains and get the necessary wood—needed for scaffoldings and similar purposes—since Judean wood is not suitable building lumber. Good building wood from Lebanon was already present from former procurements. (See Ezra 3:7.) On the 24th day of the same month the decision was taken to follow the prophet's appeal (v. 15).

Haggai's second speech was given on the 20th day of the 7th month of the same 2d year of Darius (chap. 2:1 ff.), which was one of the last days of the Feast of Tabernacles, when many people were gathered in Jerusalem. The prophet had no longer any reproaches or reproofs, but words of encouragement and beautiful promises about the great glory that should come to this second Temple. After all the preliminary work was done, a new foundation stone was laid two months later, on the 24th of the 9th month, (vs. 10, 18), and Haggai gave two speeches on that day. Commentators seem to have unanimously accepted the sequence of Haggai's activities as outlined here, up to chapter 2:9, which includes the prophet's first and second speeches. For the date of the 3d and 4th addresses various explanations have been given, which are unimportant for this study, since they do not affect the generally accepted assumption that Haggai worked with a spring-to-spring calendar.

given had the Babylonian-Persian spring-to-spring calendar as their basis.[3] This is not astonishing, since the
dates given are connected with Persian documents and
deal with official Persian affairs.

The Calendar of Ezra and Nehemiah

Clear evidence for the Jewish calendar is found
once more in the memoirs of Nehemiah. Recording in
chapter 1:1 that he had received the bad news about
the conditions in Jerusalem "in the month Chisleu, in
the twentieth year," and then had spent "days" in
weeping, fasting, and praying (v. 4), Nehemiah presented his petition to the king to be sent personally to
Jerusalem as governor "in the month Nisan, in the
twentieth year of Artaxerxes the king" (chap. 2:1).
This shows clearly that for Nehemiah, Kislev (the 9th
month) preceded Nisan (the 1st month) in the 20th
regnal year of King Artaxerxes. Many scholars have
taken this as sufficient evidence for the existence of a
fall-to-fall calendar,[4] but others have thought that a

---

[3] Esther 3:7, speaking of Haman as casting the lot to find out which date
would be the most suitable for destroying the Jews, started with "the first month,
that is, the month Nisan, in the twelfth year of king Ahasuerus, . . . from month
to month, to the twelfth month, that is, the month Adar." This text recording the
activity of a Persian official naturally refers to a spring-to-spring calendar, as the
Persians had it. When Mordecai's counteredict went out "in the third month, that
is, the month Sivan" (Esther 8:9), allowing the Jews to defend themselves when
the attack would come in "the twelfth month, which is the month Adar" (v. 12),
probably the same year and calendar system, namely the Persian, is meant, although
this is not stated. Since Mordecai was in Persian employ and the edict went out
as an official document, it could have contained nothing but dates reckoned according to the Persian calendar. Hence the data of the book of Esther provide no
evidence for the nature of the Jewish calendar used at that time.

[4] See Keil on these verses, also Judah Slotki in the *Soncino Books of the Bible:
Ezra, Nehemiah, and Esther.* Others, as Adeney in *The Expositor's Bible* and Rawlinson in the *Commentary . . . by Bishops and Other Clergy,* note that a spring
year cannot be meant, although they assume an "Asiatic" fall year or an anniversary
reckoning of the reign.

scribal error is involved.[5] If the Jews had only a spring-to-spring year as some scholars maintain, it would indeed be strange that they copied the Nehemiah passages without ever changing them or even noticing that errors were made. It would indeed be inexplicable that they would not have wondered why Nehemiah in the first two chapters placed Kislev before Nisan in year 20 of a Persian king, if they began their year with Nisan, and everyone knew that Nisan was the 1st month.

The translators of the LXX, who corrected the Bible texts in many places in their translation where they thought that the text contained inconsistencies or needed corrections, translated this text exactly as it is in Hebrew, and it has been transmitted to us without change in the Hebrew as well as in the Greek texts.

These observations make it unavoidable to conclude that in the time of Nehemiah the Jews had returned to their ancient fall-to-fall civil year as it had existed before the Exile for so many centuries. Nehemiah arrived in Judah when the nationalistic sentiments of the Jews ran high. After the humiliating experience of the Exile, the little nation had experienced a rebirth, had rebuilt its Temple, restored its religious services, and had received the right to re-establish its judiciary

---

[5] Rudolf Kittel (*Geschichte des Volkes Israel*, vol. 3, p. 616) thinks that the words "in the twentieth year" of Nch. 1:1 were mistakenly taken over from chapter 2:1. Gustave Hölscher (in *Die Heilige Schrift des Alten Testaments*, ed. by E. Kautzsch, vol. 2, p. 525) considers these words either as a gloss or as an evidence of an anniversary reckoning of Artaxerxes' regnal years. Wilhelm Rudolph (*Esra und Nehemia*, p. 102) believes that Nehemiah's original manuscript contained the words "nineteenth year of King Artaxerxes" in ch. 1:1. This phrase had then, according to Rudolph, somehow been lost in the transmission of the text, and a scribe had subsequently filled the resultant gap by copying from ch. 2:1 the words "in the twentieth year."

system under Ezra. This remarkable re-establishment of the Jews had caused a strong consciousness of national values, so that things foreign had been abandoned, like foreign languages, and probably also the Babylonian calendar, although Babylonian month names had become so much rooted that they were retained.

In the Hebrew Bible the books of Ezra and Nehemiah were regarded as one volume until A.D. 1448, in which year the presently known division was first introduced in a Hebrew manuscript. In the Greek translations the division is found since the time of Origen (3d century), and in the Latin translations since Jerome's Vulgate (5th century).[6] The book Ezra-Nehemiah therefore seems to have had a common editor, who had collected the records of the time of Zerubbabel and combined them with the memoirs of Ezra and Nehemiah in one book. This leads to the conclusion that if in the section of the book containing Nehemiah's memoirs a fall-to-fall year can be demonstrated, the same calendar would naturally apply to the section dealing with Nehemiah's contemporary, Ezra.

Summary of the Biblical Evidence

The study of the pre-exilic and postexilic records as discussed in the preceding chapter and this one shows thus that from the time of Solomon an almost consistently used civil fall-to-fall calendar can be recognized, although the records the Bible provides are meager in

---

[6] Robert H. Pfeiffer, *Introduction to the Old Testament*, p. 813; Slotki, *op. cit.*, Introduction to Ezra, p. 107.

73

Religious Year (beginning in spring)		Beginning of Jewish months according to Julian Calendar	Civil Year (beginning in fall)	
Number of the month	Name of the month		Number of the month	Name of the month
1	Nisan	March/April		
2	Iyyar	April/May		
3	Sivan	May/June		
4	Tammuz	June/July		
5	Ab	July/Aug.		
6	Elul	Aug./Sept.		
7	Tishri	Sept./Oct.	7	Tishri
8	Marcheshvan	Oct./Nov.	8	Marcheshvan
9	Kislev	Nov./Dec.	9	Kislev
10	Tebeth	Dec./Jan.	10	Tebeth
11	Shebat	Jan./Feb.	11	Shebat
12	Adar*	Feb./March	12	Adar°
		March/April	1	Nisan
		April/May	2	Iyyar
		May/June	3	Sivan
		June/July	4	Tammuz
		July/Aug.	5	Ab
		Aug./Sept.	6	Elul

° In leap years an Adar II (Hebrew <u>Ve-adar</u>) was inserted between Adar and Nisan.'

Table 1

this respect. This calendar can be demonstrated to have been in existence in the time of Solomon, during the time of the kingdom of Judah, with clear evidence from

7 Since the Mosaic regulations required the offering of a sheaf of barley one day after the Passover sabbath (Lev. 23:10-15), that festival must come at the time of the barley harvest, which in Palestine generally occurs in April. This was accomplished by the insertion of an extra month after the end of the ecclesiastical year— a second Adar between the months Adar and Nisan. Otherwise the Passover feast, which was celebrated in the middle of the month Nisan, would have come too early without such an extra month every two or three years.

Some scholars think that the ancient postexilic Jews intercalated in the same way as the Babylonians did (see pp. 45-48), namely by inserting sometimes a second Elul and at other times a second Adar. (Martin Sprengling, "Chronological Notes from the Aramaic Papyri," *AJSL*, 27, 1911, pp. 233-266.) Jewish scholars, however, have maintained that the second Elul was never used by the Jews, since the insertion of an extra month between the 6th (Elul) and the 7th month (Tishri) would have lengthened the interval between the great Jewish feasts which fell in the 1st and the 7th months of the ecclesiastical year. (D. Sidersky, "Le calendrier sémitique des papyri araméens d'Assouan," *Journal Asiatique*, series 10, vol. 16, 1910, pp. 587-592.)

the reigns of Josiah, Jehoiakim, and Jehoiachin, and after the Exile in Nehemiah's time.

The evidence in some Biblical books is ambiguous, whereas that of Haggai has generally been interpreted as showing that he used the Babylonian spring-to-spring calendar, which had probably been adopted during the Exile and possibly not replaced by the time-honored fall-to-fall national calendar until some years later.

It may be of some advantage to give the list of the Hebrew month names as they were in use after the Exile, and the approximate time of their beginning in terms of the Julian calendar. It is not superfluous to stress once more the fact that the month names for the civil as well as for the religious year were the same, and that their numbers were retained in both systems of year dating as Table 1 shows.

Extra-Biblical Evidence for the Jewish Reckoning

That the 5th century Jews actually counted the regnal years of Persian kings according to their own fall-to-fall calendar is attested not only by Nehemiah, and later on traditionally by the Talmud,[8] but also by some archeological evidence from the well-known Aramaic papyri from Elephantine.

Elephantine is a Nile island of Upper Egypt situated near the Nubian border at Assuan, the ancient Syene. During the latter part of the 19th and the early part of

---

[8] According to the explanation of Rosh Hashanah 1. 1 given by the Rabbis, the 1st of Tishri is the New Year for foreign kings. See *The Mishnah*, "Rosh Hashanah," 1. 1 (trans. H. Danby, p. 188). See also the Gemara on Rosh Hashanah 1. 1 in *The Babylonian Talmud*, "Rosh Hashanah," pp. 3a, 3b, 8a (trans. Isidore Epstein, pp. 7, 30).

the present century, papyrus scrolls were discovered on that island, some of which have only recently become known.

The first group of papyri was bought from Assuan dealers in 1904 and published in 1906.[9] Many more such documents were discovered in a systematic excavation (1906-1908) carried out on behalf of the Berlin Museum.[10] They were published in 1911.[11] In 1947 another group of papyri from the same island came to light among the personal effects of Mr. Charles Edwin Wilbour in the Brooklyn Museum. They had been bought at Elephantine in 1893 but had remained in one of Mr. Wilbour's trunks for half a century before they were rediscovered.[12] They are of the utmost importance, since they more than double the number of dated papyri hitherto available for a reconstruction of the Jewish calendar.

All these documents, dated, and undated, now totaling more than one hundred in number, are written in Aramaic, the lingua franca of the Persian empire.[13] They originate from a Jewish colony on the island of

---

[9] A. H. Sayce and A. E. Cowley, *Aramaic Papyri Discovered at Assuan.*

[10] W. Honroth, O. Rubensohn, and F. Zucker, "Bericht über die Ausgrabungen auf Elephantine in den Jahren 1906-1908," *Zeitschrift für ägyptische Sprache,* 46 (1909-1910), pp. 14-61.

[11] Eduard Sachau, *Aramäische Papyrus und Ostraka aus einer jüdischen Militär-Kolonie zu Elephantine.*

[12] Emil G. Kraeling, *The Brooklyn Museum Aramaic Papyri,* pp. 9-11.

All Elephantine papyri known up to 1923 were published by A. E. Cowley, *Aramaic Papyri of the Fifth Century B.C.* Quotations of these papyri will be taken from this work unless otherwise indicated, and the abbreviation *AP 1, 2,* etc., will be used. The more recently discovered group in the Brooklyn Museum, edited by Emil G. Kraeling, was published in 1953 under the title *The Brooklyn Museum Aramaic Papyri.* These papyri will be referred to in the present work as *Kraeling 1, 2,* etc.

[13] Raymond A. Bowman, "Arameans, Aramaic, and the Bible," *JNES,* 7 (1948), p. 90.

Elephantine. The dated documents are from the 5th century B.C., and from internal evidence it can be gathered that the undated papyri also date from the same period.[14]

These documents reveal that the Jews of Elephantine formed a garrison in this fortress of Egypt's southern border, and that they had been there for some time when Cambyses conquered the country and made it a Persian possession.[15] The papyri are also very instructive in revealing the type of polytheistic religion practiced by these Jews in Egypt, which was very similar to that found by Jeremiah when he arrived there after Jerusalem's destruction in the early 6th century B.C.[16] As contemporary source material of the time of Ezra and Nehemiah, these documents are thus of the utmost value in informing us concerning the economic, religious, and secular history of the 5th century Jewish colony in southern Egypt.

Moreover they form exceedingly important source material for the study of the calendar in use among the Jews of Elephantine during this century. Since all dated papyri are treated in Appendix 2, a summary of the important points is sufficient here.

Papyri bearing one date.—Four of the dated papyri (*AP 17, 26, 30, 31*) contain only one date each, expressed in Babylonian month names. Both the Persians and the Jews after the Exile used the Babylonian month names, but since these four documents are either

---

[14] Cowley, *op. cit.*, p. xiv.
[15] Kraeling, *op. cit.*, pp. 41-48; Cowley, *op. cit.*, p. xvi.
[16] Cowley, *op. cit.*, pp. xviii, xix; *cf.* Jer. 44.

addressed to or issued by Persian officials, the assumption seems to be warranted that all dates are Persian, and that the Persian way of reckoning is employed for these four documents.

A number of documents bear only the Egyptian date.[17] The dating of these papyri creates no problems, since Egyptian dates of this period can always be converted into their Julian equivalents with certainty, as has been explained in connection with the Egyptian calendar. Only the uncertain readings in some of the documents, and doubt about the kings referred to in others, make it impossible to reach finality in the dating of all papyri bearing only the Egyptian date.

Papyri dated in two calendars.—Twenty-two of the papyri bear double dates.[18] Since these papyri were written when Egypt was a Persian province, they are dated in terms of the regnal years of the Persian kings, but give the month and day in both the Semitic lunar calendar and the Egyptian solar one. This enables us to convert the Semitic dates into their B.C. equivalents, because the Egyptian New Year's Day for every year of the Persian period is known.[19] The date line is poorly preserved in some of them, and scribal mistakes are involved evidently in some others, which make them unfit witnesses; yet 14 papyri can be used to reconstruct the Jewish calendar in use in Elephantine in the 5th century B.C. The earliest of these typical double-dated

---

[17] *AP* 1, 2, 7, 22, 29, 35, 43; *Kraeling* 11, 12, 13.

[18] *AP* 5, 6, 8, 9, 10, 13, 14, 15, 20, 25, 28; *Kraeling* 1, 2, 3, 4, 5, 6, 7, 8, 9, 10, 14.

[19] See footnote 2, p. 129. The dates of these double-dated papyri are discussed in detail in Appendix 2.

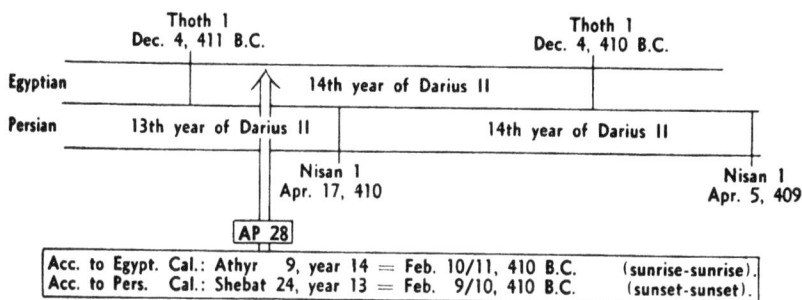

Thoth 1 Dec. 4, 411 B.C.		Thoth 1 Dec. 4, 410 B.C.	
Egyptian	14th year of Darius II		
Persian	13th year of Darius II	14th year of Darius II	
	Nisan 1 Apr. 17, 410	Nisan 1 Apr. 5, 409	

AP 28

Acc. to Egypt. Cal.: Athyr 9, year 14 = Feb. 10/11, 410 B.C.	(sunrise-sunrise).
Acc. to Pers. Cal.: Shebat 24, year 13 = Feb. 9/10, 410 B.C.	(sunset-sunset).

Fig. 3

papyri (*AP 5*) has the following date line: "On the 18th of Elul [in a calendar using Babylonian month names], that is the 28th day of Pachons [in the Egyptian calendar], year 15 of King Xerxes."

Non-Persian reckoning of regnal years.—Two of the afore-mentioned papyri (*AP 25, 28*) show clearly how complicated the dating was during that part of the year when the two calendar years did not coincide. The date line of each carries *two* regnal years. Both of these documents were written in the reign of Darius II, when the Egyptian calendar year began about four months earlier than the Persian. *AP 28*, for example, was a double-dated papyrus written in February, 410 B.C., in the latter part of Darius' year 13 according to the spring-beginning Persian calendar. But in Egypt, with the new calendar year, a new regnal year had already begun on Thoth I in the preceding December. Hence the date formula, expressed in terms of both calendars, gives both regnal years, 13 and 14, for the same date.[20] This will be explained with the help of Figure 3.

---

[20] It may seem strange to the modern reader that a single event was dated in two different years, but such a procedure was common even in Colonial America,

The date line of the papyrus reads: "On the 24th of Shebat, year 13, that is the 9th day of Athyr, year 14 of Darius." [21] The first date, using the month name Shebat (which could be in either the Jewish or the Persian calendar) [22] has the year number 13, one less than the number 14 after the Egyptian month Athyr. The 9th of Athyr, the 3d month of the Egyptian civil calendar, fell in 410 B.C. on February 10, more than two months before the Babylonian-Persian New Year, Nisan 1 (April 17). The Egyptians began Darius II's year 14 on their own New Year, Thoth 1 (Dec. 4, 411 B.C.), 4½ months before the Persians did. [23] Therefore any event occurring between those new-year days would be dated in year 14 by the Egyptians and year 13 by the Persians.

Evidently the Egyptians under Persian rule were

---

before the Gregorian calendar was adopted by England in 1752. At that time the British, with their "Old Style" (Julian) calendar, were of course 11 days out of step with the "New Style" (Gregorian) calendar then in use in the western European countries. (See footnote 25 in chapter 2.) Further, from January 1 through March 24 the year number on British documents was one lower than the Gregorian number, or else appeared in a double form such as 1721/2, etc. This year difference had nothing to do with the 11-day correction, but resulted from the fact that the British had retained a medieval custom of beginning the year on March 25, "Lady Day," nearly 3 months later than the original January 1.

For example, George Washington was born 20 years before the English countries adopted the Gregorian calendar. Thus Washington's birth record in his family Bible reads "ye 11th Day of February 1731/2." (Facsimile, frontispiece in Douglas Southall Freeman, *George Washington*, vol. 1.) It was February 11, Old Style (O.S.), which later became February 22, New Style (N.S.); and the year 1731 was still running by English official reckoning until March 24, although in the countries using the Gregorian calendar the year 1732 had already begun on January 1.

[21] Cowley, *op. cit.*, p. 104.

[22] For evidence that the non-Egyptian date here is Jewish and not Persian, see pp. 84-89. For the subject discussed here, however, this is of no importance.

[23] During the fifth century B.C. this interval was about 3 to 4½ months. While Nisan 1 never fell earlier than March, Thoth 1 moved back from Dec. 26 in 500 B.C. to Dec. 1 in 401. It had fallen on Dec. 26 in 501, 500, 499, and 498; on Dec. 25 the next four years, and so on; see p. 38. (For R. A. Parker's theory that the Egyptians while under Persian rule adjusted their numbering so as to begin the Egyptian year 1 always on Thoth 1 preceding the Persian year 1, see p. 173, note 30.)

not required to conform to the dating system of their overlords, but in their own legal practices were allowed to use their national calendar. The two papyri mentioned show that they used their solar calendar as well as their own system of reckoning the years of the Persian kings, although this practice resulted in their year numbers being different from those used by the Persians during part of every year.

Further, it seems that the Egyptian date was ordinarily required for legal purposes in Egypt. Nearly all papyri that contain legal documents bear either the Egyptian date only or two dates, one of which is Egyptian; thus the conclusion is valid that legal documents were normally required to bear the Egyptian date.[24] Furthermore, it can be observed that in the majority of double-dated papyri (18 against 2) which give only one year number, the regnal year number of the Persian king immediately follows the Egyptian month date.

That the year number is really the one according to the Egyptian reckoning, and not according to the Persian reckoning, can be demonstrated in several cases showing that the double dates agree only if the year number is taken to represent the Egyptian way of reckoning the regnal years of Persian kings. For example, papyrus *Kraeling 10* synchronizes the 20th of Adar with the 8th of Choiak in the 3d year of Artaxerxes II. The two mentioned dates coincided on March 9, 402

---

[24] Parker questions the validity of this reasoning (in his "Some Considerations on the Nature of the Fifth-Century Jewish Calendar at Elephantine," *JNES*, 14 [1955], p. 271), but his arguments are not convincing to the present authors.

B.C., which was Choiak 8 in the 3d year of Artaxerxes II according to Egyptian reckoning but Adar 20 in the 2d year of Artaxerxes II according to the Persian reckoning. A year later, when Adar 20 of Artaxerxes II's 3d year according to Persian reckoning fell on March 28, 401 B.C., no synchronism can be achieved, since Choiak 8 was March 8 in that year. This shows clearly that the Egyptian regnal system was usually used in the papyri that record only one figure for the regnal year.

Second regnal year sometimes omitted.—In the papyri *AP 25* and *28* the scribes were careful enough to give the two variant year numbers, as was already explained above. This they should always have done in that portion of the year when a difference between the two calendar systems was involved; but it seems to have been felt that it was not always necessary, since everyone knew that the regnal year number of the king was higher by 1 according to the Egyptian reckoning during that portion of the year that fell between Thoth 1 and the next Persian New Year in the spring (or the Jewish New Year in the fall)—the sequence shown in Figure 3 (p. 79). This sequence is found in the papyri in the period from Xerxes to Artaxerxes II, and possibly throughout the Persian period. The difference between *AP 25* and *AP 10* shows clearly that the scribe who wrote the first had the habit of giving the regnal year numbers according to two systems, but the other failed to do this. These two papyri, although written in different years, are both dated in the same months—Kislev and Thoth—but only *AP 25* says that Kislev 3 fell in the year 8, and Thoth 12 in the year 9 of Darius II. The other, *AP 10,* simply states that Kislev 7 is Thoth 4 in the 9th year of Artaxerxes (I). If it were as specific as *AP 25,* it should read Kislev 7 in year 8 is Thoth 4 in year 9 of Artaxerxes. Thus the absence of the second year number does not mean that the year is the same in both calendars.

Calendar not determined by month names.—Since the Egyptian dating on these papyri seems to be the customary legal form, the addition of a lunar-calendar date is evidently optional, allowed for the convenience of the Jewish colonists who were parties to the legal transactions recorded. In that case we should expect those dates to be Jewish rather than Persian. But the fact that Babylonian month names are used is no proof that the calendar involved was Persian, since both the Persians and the postexilic Jews employed the Babylonian month names. The Jewish calendar showed some variations from that of the Babylonians,[25] but these variations are only small, involving usually a difference of only one day, as will be shown in the study of the Elephantine papyri in Appendix 2. Furthermore, the Jews apparently intercalated a second Adar only, and not, like the Babylonians, an occasional second Elul, which would have lengthened the interval between the Jewish feasts of the 1st month and the 7th

---

[25] No harmony between the double dates can be achieved in many cases, as Parker's study shows, unless the fact is admitted that the Jews after the Exile did not adopt the Babylonian calendar part and parcel. In his discussion of 7 double-dated papyri, agreement to the day was reached in only one case, because the dates of the Babylonian calendar were applied (Parker, "Persian and Egyptian Chronology," *AJSL,* 58 [1941], pp. 288-292).

month. However, the accuracy of this view, shared by a number of scholars, cannot be conclusively proved, for although 32 of the 37 embolismic months of the Babylonian calendar in the 5th century B.C. have been attested by actual cuneiform tablets,[26] not enough Jewish texts are available to indicate how the Jews intercalated during this time.

Evidence for fall-to-fall calendar.—The evidence for the fact that the Jews in Upper Egypt, like Nehemiah in Palestine, counted the regnal years of Persian kings according to their civil fall-to-fall calendar was found only recently when the Brooklyn Museum papyri became available. Before that time the two already mentioned papyri (*AP 25* and *28*), each of which carries a date line giving two year numbers, were the only proofs that the Jews used two systems of numbering the regnal years of Persian kings. Those papyri did not make it clear whether the non-Egyptian system was the Persian or the Jewish one, because both documents date from a period of the year—the interval between Tishri 1 and Nisan 1—when the regnal numbers according to the Persian and the Jewish systems were the same. Only a regnal numbering that fits one type of year and excludes the other could solve the problem.

The papyrus providing the evidence for the existence of the fall-to-fall calendar among the Elephantine Jews is *Kraeling 6*. This important document, written early in Darius' reign, contains the following date line:

---

[26] Parker and Dubberstein, *Babylonian Chronology* (1956), pp. 6-9, 30-33.

"On the 8th of Pharmuthi, which is the 8th day of Tammuz, year 3 of Darius, the king." With the exception of one other document (*Kraeling 1*), it is the only one with a date line showing the peculiarity of presenting the Egyptian date first, and then the date using the Babylonian month name, which is followed by the regnal year of king Darius II. All other double-dated papyri have the Egyptian month date in the second place, next to the year number. The unusual procedure found in *Kraeling 6* was apparently the reason that the scribe, instead of giving the commonly used Egyptian regnal year for Darius II, naturally added to the Jewish month and day the regnal year by Jewish reckoning, as the following discussion will demonstrate.

Before showing how this papyrus fits into the picture of the Jewish fall-to-fall calendar, we shall, with the help of Figure 4 on page 86, fix the different systems used to count Darius II's regnal years.

The death of Artaxerxes I and the accession of his son, Darius II, to the throne must have occurred by February, 423 B.C., since the last known tablet dated in Artaxerxes I's reign and the first one of Darius II were both written in February, 423 B.C.[27] The accession year of Darius, according to the Persian reckoning, thus lasted to the following New Year's Day, Nisan 1, which fell on April 11, 423 B.C., according to the Babylonian calendar used by the Persians.

In the Egyptian civil calendar, however, a new year had begun on the previous Thoth 1, which fell on Dec.

---

[27] *Ibid.*, p. 18.

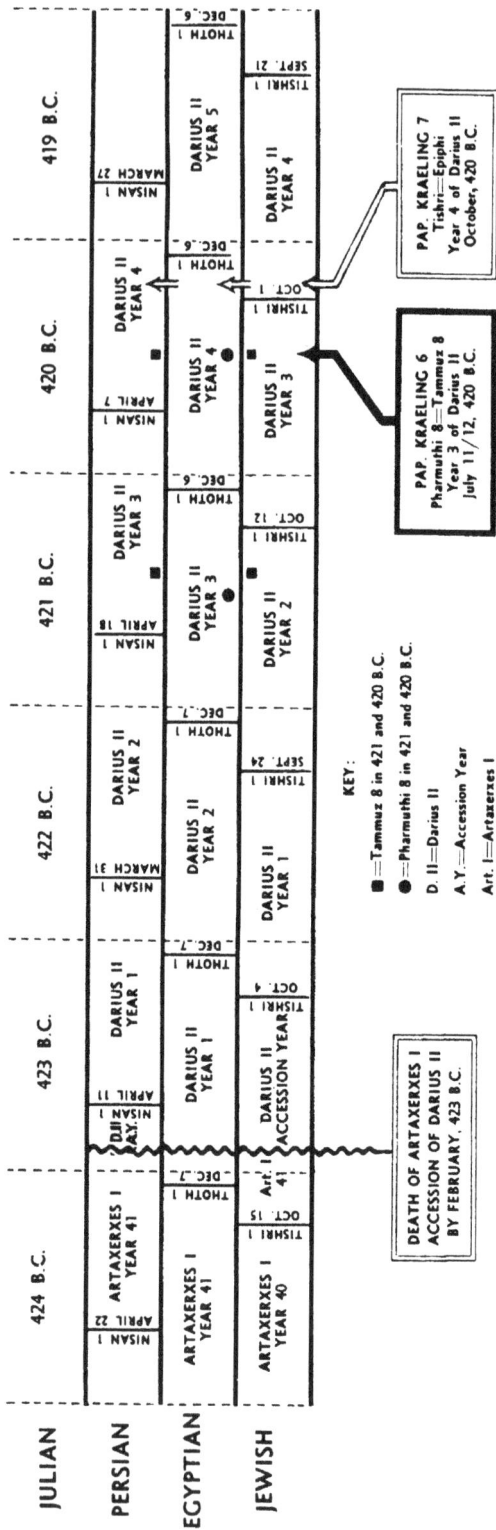

Fig. 4

The Use of the Jewish Fall-to-Fall Calendar Illustrated by Papyrus *Kraeling 6*

The double month dates of *Kraeling 6* coincided only in 420 B.C., and could be dated in the third year of Darius II only according to the Jewish fall-to-fall year. No harmony can be achieved in the third year of Darius in either the Egyptian or the Persian reckoning.

7, 424 B.C. The year beginning on that date is the 325th of the Nabonassar era, marked in Ptolemy's Canon as the 1st year of Darius II. Since the Egyptians could not know the death date of Artaxerxes I before it occurred, they must have dated all documents after Dec. 7, 424 B.C., in the 42d regnal year of Artaxerxes I until they heard of his death. Then upon news of Darius II's accession they began to date documents in the 1st year of Darius.[28] If they had called it the accession year instead, then the 1st Egyptian year would have begun in December, 423, 9 months later than the Persian 1st year. However, the double year dating in papyri *AP 25* and *28*, which come from the same reign, prove that the Egyptian year ran earlier than the corresponding Persian year.

If the Jews, however, used a fall-to-fall civil calendar, they counted the accession year of Darius from February, 423 B.C., until their next New Year's Day, Tishri 1, which fell on October 4, 423 B.C. Figure 4 shows graphically the various systems in use under Darius in their relationship to the Julian calendar.

How then does papyrus *Kraeling 6* fit into the picture? It was dated in the 3d year of Darius II, on the 8th day of the Egyptian month Pharmuthi, which in that year was the 8th day of Tammuz (a Persian or Jewish month) that came in midsummer. Figure 4 shows that the 3d year of Darius II in both Persian and Egyptian

---

[28] The papyrus *AP 6*, to be discussed on pp. 100, 101, also provides a dating in a transition year, since it mentions the 21st year (the death year) of Xerxes in connection with the accession of Artaxerxes I.

calendars includes the summer of 421 B.C., but that by the Jewish reckoning, his year 3 did not begin until the fall of 421, and so included the summer of 420 instead. Thus we can see that if this papyrus was written in the summer of 421, it could have been dated in year 3 according to either the Persian or the Egyptian calendars, but if it was written in 420, its year 3 could be reckoned only according to the Jewish calendar. Therefore we need to determine in which of these two summers Pharmuthi 8 and Tammuz 8 fell on the same day.

In 421 B.C. Pharmuthi 8 was July 11/12 and Tammuz 8 was July 22/23; this year is obviously impossible. But in 420, Pharmuthi fell again on July 11/12 (sunrise to sunrise), whereas Tammuz 8 was July 11/12 (sunset to sunset). Consequently it can be seen that this document must have been written in 420 B.C., and that therefore the scribe *must have been using the Jewish fall-to-fall calendar.*

One more papyrus, *Kraeling 7*, should be mentioned in this connection, since it fits into the picture set forth here. It was written three months after the last-discussed document, "in the month Tishri, that is Epiphi, year 4 of Darius." After the 1st of Tishri, the Jewish New Year's Day, all three systems of reckoning, the Persian, Egyptian, and Jewish, were in harmony for several months, as can be seen from Figure 4. Therefore the year number given in this papyrus was the same 4th year (in Tishri which coincided approximately with Epiphi in 420 B.C.) according to all three aforementioned systems.

THE POSTEXILIC JEWISH CALENDAR

This document throws some additional light on papyrus *Kraeling 6* and agrees with the conclusions derived from it. *Kraeling 6*, however, is the important extra-Biblical witness (1) for the existence of a fall-to-fall civil calendar among the Jews in Elephantine in the 5th century B.C., and (2) for the fact that the Jews there counted the regnal years of a Persian king according to this fall-to-fall calendar in the same way as Nehemiah had done a few years earlier (Neh. 1:1; 2:1).

Scholars who do not believe in the existence of such a regnal-year reckoning or of a civil fall-to-fall calendar among the Jews during that time will declare that the scribe of the papyrus *Kraeling 6* made a mistake.[29] Similarly scholars have charged the Nehemiah passages with being erroneous, since these verses do not agree with the theory that the Jews of that time had adopted the Babylonian spring-to-spring calendar.

Instead of declaring the Nehemiah passages and this papyrus from Elephantine as mistakes, it is more reasonable to see in them independent evidence supporting each other. Both documents come from the same age—one of them being extant in its original form—and were written by people who belonged to the same religious group. Hence it seems that their strong and united testimony should outweigh the theory of seeing mistakes in their dates.

---

[29] Parker considers the year 3 of *Kraeling 6* to be an error for year 4 and consequently recommends an emendation, *JNES*, 14 (1955), p. 274.

Conclusion.—The results reached from a study of the Elephantine papyri discussed so far, can be summarized under the following five points:

(1) The Egyptians used no accession year unless they did so in special cases (see p. 173, note 30), but began to reckon the 1st regnal year of Darius II with Thoth 1 preceding the 1st Persian regnal year, which began with Nisan 1. Thus the beginning of each Egyptian regnal year of Darius preceded the Persian one by several months (*AP 25, 28*).

(2) The Jews in Egypt were not bound to use the Persian calendar in reckoning the years of a Persian king's reign, but employed their own system of reckoning besides the legal Egyptian one (*AP 25, 28*).

(3) The absence of a second regnal year number in documents coming from that portion of the year when differences existed is no proof that such a difference was not recognized (*AP 10*).

(4) The months following a king's death until the next Jewish New Year's Day were considered as the new king's accession year (*Kraeling 6, AP 25, 28*).

(5) The Jews employed a civil fall-to-fall calendar beginning with Tishri 1 as New Year's Day (*Kraeling 6*).

The Chronology of Ezra 7

The Biblical Artaxerxes

The chronological sequence of Ezra and Nehemiah.
—The books of Ezra and Nehemiah, which formed one
book in the Hebrew Bible until very recent times,[1] tell
the story of the restoration of the Jews, under three
successive leaders—Zerubbabel, Ezra, and Nehemiah.
The historical accuracy of this sequence was generally
accepted among Jews and Christians alike until the
end of the last century. However, since 1890 the situation has changed markedly. It was in that year that
the Belgian scholar A. Van Hoonacker brought out
his first study on the chronological order of Ezra and
Nehemiah, in which he argued for a reversing of the
traditional order, making Ezra one of the successors of
Nehemiah.

This is not the place to discuss the pros and cons
of this theory, which a growing number of scholars
have accepted during the past 75 years.[2] It should be

---

[1] See the remarks made on p. 73 of the present work.

[2] H. H. Rowley, although differing in his conclusions from the present authors,
furnishes in his work on the subject ("The Chronological Order of Ezra and
Nehemiah," in his *The Servant of the Lord and Other Essays on the Old Testament*,
pp. 135-168), an almost exhaustive survey of the history of this problem with a
good discussion of the arguments advanced on both sides, and an excellent bibliog-
raphy of the subject in the footnotes.

stated that an impressive number of scholars still adhere to the traditional view that Ezra came to Judea 13 years before Nehemiah, and was later associated in Nehemiah's work.[3] This shows that the arguments brought up in favor of a later activity of Ezra have not been strong enough to convince all critical scholars of the soundness of the theory that Ezra arrived in Palestine after Nehemiah, either in the last years of Artaxerxes I or in the 7th year of Artaxerxes II.

That this modern theory has not been universally accepted should be well remembered in view of occasional claims that Van Hoonacker's date for Ezra's arrival "may now be said to be virtually certain,"[4] or that "recent scholarship would put the journey of Ezra to Palestine" in "the seventh year of Artaxerxes II."[5]

The Artaxerxes of Nehemiah.—Doubts as to which Artaxerxes is meant in the book of Nehemiah have almost completely disappeared since the discovery of the Elephantine papyri. The evidence contained in some of these papyri virtually establishes the fact that Nehemiah held his office as governor of Judea under Artaxerxes I.

From the Elephantine papyri *AP 30* and *31* we learn that Johanan was high priest in Jerusalem in 407 B.C.[6] He is mentioned in Nehemiah 12:22, 23 (*cf.* also Ezra 10:6) as the son of the high priest Eliashib, who held his office under Nehemiah (Neh. 3:1).

[3] *Ibid.*, pp. 138, 141, 142.
[4] Albright, *From the Stone Age to Christianity*, p. 248.
[5] Kraeling, "New Light on the Elephantine Colony," *The Biblical Archaeologist*, 15 (1952), p. 66.
[6] See Cowley, *op. cit.*, pp. 114, 121.

Josephus, however, claims that Johanan was the grandson of Eliashib.[7] Whether or not he is right is irrelevant to our argument, since we are interested to find that according to both sources, the Bible and Josephus, the high priest Eliashib of Nehemiah's time preceded the high priest of 407 B.C., Johanan. This makes Nehemiah a man of the former generation under Artaxerxes I.

Additional evidence comes from the mention, in one of these documents, of "Delaiah and Shelemiah, the sons of Sanballat governor of Samaria" (*AP 30,* line 29), showing that Sanballat, the most bitter foe of Nehemiah, was still governor of Judea's neighboring province, Samaria, in 407 B.C. Although the Bible does not tell us that he held the office of governor, it shows clearly that he was a person of influence, and there is nothing in the narrative as told by Nehemiah that is inconsistent with his being governor. It seems, however, that in 407 B.C. he was an old man, and had transferred the administration of the state to his sons, since the Jews in Egypt placed their requests before them. The time when Sanballat decided affairs alone seems to have been a thing of the past, and since the work of Nehemiah clearly lay in the period when Sanballat was actively in charge of the affairs of state in his province, it becomes rather evident that the only Artaxerxes under whom Nehemiah could have served was Artaxerxes I. For these and some less weighty reasons, few scholars of the past half century have doubted this.

---

[7] Josephus *Antiquities* xi. 7.1 (Loeb ed., vol. 6, p. 457).

The Artaxerxes of Ezra 7.—The placing of Nehemiah in the time of Artaxerxes I is now quite certain.[8]
If we accept the unity of the books of Ezra and Nehemiah, and also the sequence of the story as given in
these books, then Artaxerxes I must be considered the
one who gave the permission to Ezra for his return to
Palestine and the reform of the judicial system, as described in Ezra 7. In that case Ezra came to Palestine in
the 7th year of Artaxerxes I (Ezra 7:7-9) and carried
out his assignment. Then there is silence in the Bible
about his further activities until we find him participat-
ing in the dedication of the walls of Jerusalem in the
time of Nehemiah, at least 13 years later (Neh. 5:14),
as one of the two leaders of the thanksgiving proces-
sions marching on top of the completed walls (Neh.
12:36). Again he appears as one of the leading men
when the law was read and the covenant made between
the people and God under his and Nehemiah's spon-
sorship (Neh. 8:9).

These considerations make it imperative to accept
Artaxerxes I as the king under whom first Ezra and
then Nehemiah worked for their nation. Any reversal

---

[8] The 1962 discovery of a group of Samaritan papyri in a cave in the Wâdî
Dâliyeh, about 9 miles north of Jericho, has provided evidence for the existence of
three governors of Samaria named Sanballat during the 5th and 4th centuries B.C.
See Frank M. Cross, Jr., "The Discovery of the Samaria Papyri," *The Biblical
Archaeologist*, 26 (1963), pp. 110-121. This discovery has resolved an apparent
difficulty: Nehemiah's records, supported by the Elephantine Papyrus *AP 30*, placed
Sanballat in the time of Artaxerxes I and Darius II, but Josephus (*Antiquities*,
xi. 7.2, 8.4), mentioned Sanballat in the time of Darius III and Alexander. Now it
is known that both Nehemiah and Josephus were right. Some scholars had already,
before the *Dâliyeh* discovery, considered the possibility of two Sanballats controlling
Samaria. C. C. Torrey, for example ("Sanballat 'the Horonite,' " *Journal of Biblical
Literature*, 47 [1928], pp. 380-389), suggested two Sanballats, two generations apart,
with Nehemiah a contemporary of the later Sanballat—a view not supported by the
new discoveries.

in this sequence does violence to the narrative of the two books as they have been transmitted to us, and has therefore to be rejected. In accepting Artaxerxes I as the king of Ezra 7 we are in good company with the majority of scholars who have so far expressed themselves on the subject.[9]

The Regnal Years of Artaxerxes I

Ezra, like his postexilic predecessors and the later-coming Nehemiah, dated events according to the regnal years of Persian kings under whom they lived. Most scholars assume that these dates are reckoned according to the Babylonian calendar, which was used by the Persians. The first task is therefore to ascertain the regnal years of Artaxerxes I according to the Persian calendar.

It has been shown that the Egyptians, also under Persian rule at that time, numbered the years of their Persian overlords according to the Egyptian calendar; also that our extra-Biblical evidence for the Jewish calendar, and their system of reckoning the regnal years of Persian rulers, is found in a series of documents from Egypt. Several of these bear Jewish and Egyptian dates, and one of them is our earliest date for the reign of Artaxerxes I. Therefore we must also establish the years of Artaxerxes in Egyptian reckoning.

Finally the years of Artaxerxes according to Hebrew reckoning must be ascertained.

---

[9] Rowley, *op. cit.*, pp. 143, 144.

Establishment of Persian regnal years.—The discoveries of the last hundred years made in Mesopotamia and Egypt have produced much material that has put the chronology of the Neo-Babylonian and Persian empires on a solid basis. Thousands of dated tablets, for example, can be fitted into an almost complete series of regnal years. But, as has been explained,[10] a date formula like "on the 1st day of the 5th month in the 16th year of Xerxes" is a relative statement; it means different things in different dating systems, depending on the exact date of accession, the use of the accession-year or non-accession-year system, and the different starting points of the various calendar years. In order to pin down these regnal-year series in absolute chronology, we depend on certain specific documents that furnish additional data of the sort that enable us to locate exact B.C. dates—such information as synchronisms with other dating systems, or astronomical data that can be verified by calculation.

One of these anchor points, from which we can locate other relative dates, is furnished by an astronomical tablet bearing a series of observations dated in the 37th year of Nebuchadnezzar. These fix the year as having begun on April 22/23, 568 B.C., and ended on April 11/12, 567 B.C.[11] Another astronomical tablet of equal importance has established that the 7th year of Cambyses lasted from April 6/7, 523, to March 25/26,

---

[10] See pp. 15-22.
[11] Neugebauer and Weidner, *op. cit.*, pp. 66, 67, 72.

522 B.C.[12] With the help of the canon of Ptolemy [13] and thousands of dated cuneiform documents written on clay tablets, which agree throughout as to the total of regnal years for each king, it is possible to arrive at exact dates for each of the kings reigning in the period between the two astronomical tablets. For the kings succeeding Cambyses, and especially those of the 5th century, our chronology again depends on Ptolemy's Canon and the Saros Tablets,[14] supported by numerous dated cuneiform documents, to which can be added the double-dated papyri from Elephantine, whose synchronisms between the known Egyp-

---

[12] J. N. Strassmaier, *Inschriften von Cambyses, König von Babylon*, no. 400. For the calculation of the dates of the astronomical events, see Franz X. Kugler, *Sternkunde und Sterndienst in Babel*, vol. 1, pp. 61-75. An eclipse mentioned on this tablet (see A. T. Olmstead, *History of the Persian Empire*, p. 202, for a translation of the entry) is recorded also by Ptolemy (*Almagest* v. 14, p. 172). For the time of this eclipse see Oppolzer, *Syzygien-Tafeln*, p. 31, and his *Canon der Finsternisse*, p. 335; also C. F. Lehman and F. K. Ginzel, "Die babylonisch-assyrischen Finsternisse," in Ginzel, *Spezieller Kanon der Sonnen- und Mondfinsternisse*, p. 258. The agreement between the tablet and the *Almagest* on the date of this eclipse shows that Ptolemy's numbering of Cambyses' regnal years harmonizes with the ancient Babylonian practice.

[13] See pp. 40-42 of the present work.

[14] The ancient Babylonians discovered that after 223 lunar months or about 18 years both solar and lunar eclipses repeat themselves almost exactly. Such a cycle of 18 years was called a "saros," a term which has been adopted by modern astronomers and is now used by them in the same sense. Cuneiform tablets written under the Seleucid kings and containing a list of the saros cycles have been found. For the Persian period, these Saros Tablets give, for example, the following years:

9th (year of) Darius [I]	18 (years)
27th (year of) Darius [I]	18 (years)
9th (year of) Xerxes	18 (years)
6th (year of) Artaxerxes [I]	18 (years)
24th (year of) Artaxerxes [I]	18 (years)
1st (year of) Darius [II]	18 (years) and so on.

The lengths of reign of the various kings can thus be easily determined. If, for example, 18 years elapsed between the 27th year of Darius I and the 9th year of Xerxes, Darius' reign must have had a total length of 36 years, and if 18 years lay between the 9th year of Xerxes and the 6th year of Artaxerxes I, Xerxes must have reigned altogether 21 years. Since the regnal years of kings as derived from the Saros Tablets agree in each case with those given in Ptolemy's Canon, one serves as check on the other and supports the data provided by the other. See J. N. Strassmaier, "Einige chronologische Daten aus astronomischen Rechnungen," *Zeitschrift für Assyriologie*, 7 (1892), pp. 197-204; also his "Zur Chronologie der Seleuciden," *ibid.*, 8 (1893), pp. 106-113.

tian calendar and lunar month and day furnish contemporary evidence for the regnal years of this period.[15]

For example, one of these papyri, *AP 5*, helps thus to fix the 15th regnal year of Xerxes, in which the papyrus is dated, for the double dates show that it was written between Sept. 12, sunrise, and Sept. 13, sunrise, 471 B.C.[16] Since we know that the Persian calendar year began in the spring, the 15th regnal year of Xerxes must have been the year 471/70 B.C., spring to spring. Other double-dated papyri similarly fix the B.C. dating of the accession year and 14th, 16th, 19th, 25th, 28th, 31st, and 38th regnal years of Artaxerxes I; the 3d, 8th, and 13th years of Darius II; and the 1st and 3d years of Artaxerxes II. Since the dates obtained from these papyri are in agreement with those given in Ptolemy's Canon, with which the Saros Tablets harmonize also, no reasonable doubt exists as to the validity of the accepted dates for the Persian kings of the 5th century B.C. as they are given, for instance, in Parker and Dubberstein's *Babylonian Chronology*.

The Accession of Artaxerxes I [17]

The evidence of the double-dated papyri, Ptolemy's Canon, and the Saros Tablets leads thus to the incontrovertible fact that Xerxes' reign ended in his 21st

---

[15] See pp. 75-78, and the more detailed discussion in Appendix 2.
[16] See Appendix 2, p. 135.
[17] The discussion of the Greek and later sources with regard to *AP 6* on the events surrounding Artaxerxes' accession to the throne owes much to the careful and penetrating study of Julia Neuffer, ''The Accession of Artaxerxes I,'' *AUSS*, 6 (1968), pp. 60-87.

regnal year, which began in the spring of 465 B.C., and that Artaxerxes' 1st regnal year began in the spring of 464 B.C. Thus it is equally certain that Artaxerxes' accession to the throne took place in the year 465/64 B.C. (spring to spring), the year in which his father had died.

This information is not sufficient to indicate how dates in this reign were reckoned in the Egyptian calendar year (beginning in December) and in the Jewish regnal year (beginning in the autumn). It is necessary to know in which of three periods of the year the king came to the throne: (1) between the Persian and Jewish New Year's days, (2) between the Jewish and Egyptian New Year's days, or (3) between the Egyptian and Persian New Year's days.

Unfortunately no contemporary dated cuneiform tablets from Xerxes' last year or from Artaxerxes' accession year have so far come to light. And such texts are needed to establish the death date of Xerxes and the date of accession of his son within the Persian year 465/64 B.C. The latest known tablet from Xerxes' reign comes from his 20th year,[18] and the earliest dated tablet from Artaxerxes I comes from the 3d month of his 1st year.[19]

Ur tablet formerly relied on.—For a while it was thought that a cuneiform tablet found in the excava-

---

[18] Parker and Dubberstein, *Babylonian Chronology* (1956), p. 17, mentioning an unpublished text from Persepolis (Oriental Institute A 23253) which refers to the 10th-12th months of Xerxes' 20th year.
[19] *Ibid.*, referring to an unpublished text in Teheran, Iran (PT 4 441).

tion campaign of 1930-31 in Ur provided the desired answer. Containing an agreement dealing with the re-arrangement of land parcels among four brothers, it is dated in the 13th year of Artaxerxes I, but states that the original arrangement was signed in the 21st year of Xerxes. H. H. Figulla, the editor of this text, inter-preted the broken remains of cuneiform characters pre-ceding the latter year number as the remnants of the month name Kislimu.[20] When in 1953 there came to light a cuneiform tablet of the Hellenistic period (to be discussed below) which dated Xerxes' death in August 465, Figulla re-evaluated his previous reading of the Ur tablet and abandoned his former published interpreta-tion.[21]

This means that the Ur tablet can no longer be used as evidence that Xerxes was still living in Decem-ber, 465, as was done in the first edition of the present work.[22]

Document of Artaxerxes' accession year.—The only document extant written in the accession year of Ar-taxerxes is an Aramaic papyrus (*AP 6*) from the Jewish colony of Elephantine, in Egypt, written on Jan. 2/3, 464 B.C. It begins with the following date line: "On the 18th of Kislev, which is the [17th] day of Thoth, in year 21, the beginning of reign when King Artaxerxes

---

[20] H. H. Figulla, *Ur Excavations; Texts, IV: Business Documents*, no. 193, p. 15. He does not print the text or translate it but describes it thus: "193. Re-arrangement of land parcels (first arrangement: Kislimu, 21st year of Xerxes): Artaxerxes I, ?. 4. 13."

[21] By letter of May 5, 1954, to S. H. Horn.

[22] See pp. 101-105 of the first edition of the present work, where this text was used as evidence that Xerxes had not died, and that Artaxerxes had not come to the throne, earlier than December, 465, since Kislimu began in that month.

sat on his throne." [23] It is certain that this document was written in the accession year [24] of Artaxerxes I, and not of Artaxerxes II or III, since only this king came to the throne in the 21st year of his predecessor. [25] Unfortunately the day number of the month Thoth is broken. The remaining signs of that number could be restored to 7, 14, or 17 on paleographic grounds, [26] but only the 17th of Thoth harmonizes with the 18th of Kislev in the death year of Xerxes, which was at the same time the accession year of his son Artaxerxes; so that the restored date "17th day of Thoth" seems to be assured. The 17th of Thoth fell on Jan. 2/3, 464 B.C., sunrise to sunrise. It is thus clear that by that date the news of Artaxerxes' accession had reached Egypt, although it does not give an indication of how long before that the accession had taken place. From the unusual mention of the 21st year (of Xerxes) it was considered plausible to assume that this event had only recently happened. It was felt that the scribe had been in the habit of dating documents in the 21st year of Xerxes for so long that he began to do it in this document, but when he realized that a new king was on the throne, he finished the date line by adding the year of

---

[23] Translated from the Aramaic. See Cowley, *op. cit.*, p. 16, for the Aramaic text.

[24] See footnote 20 on p. 137. It is shown there that the term literally translated "beginning of reign" has the meaning "accession year."

[25] Artaxerxes I succeeded Xerxes, who reigned 21 years; Artaxerxes II succeeded Darius II, who reigned 19 years; Artaxerxes III succeeded Artaxerxes II, who reigned 46 years. The lengths of these reigns are attested by Ptolemy's Canon and the Saros Tablets; those of Xerxes and Darius II are corroborated by the double-dated Aramaic papyri.

[26] See pp. 135-139 and Fig. 11, p. 140.

Artaxerxes' accession.[27] That another, perhaps more plausible, explanation for this unusual date line can be given will be shown later.

A Hellenistic tablet assigns a date.—When the 3d edition of Parker and Dubberstein's *Babylonian Chronology* (extended to A.D. 75) was published in 1956, reference was made to an unpublished eclipse text in the British Museum which seems to fix the death of Xerxes by murder early in August, 465.[28] However, it has to be remembered that this text is no contemporary document, but dates from the Hellenistic period and thus was written, at the earliest, almost a century and a half after the event to which it refers. On the other hand, it may be a much younger text, which means that in that case much more than a century and a half, perhaps several centuries, separated the writer from the

---

[27] See Parker and Dubberstein, *Babylonian Chronology, 626 B.C.-A.D. 45* (2d ed., 1946), p. 16, for this interpretation in a similar case.

[28] The text in question is briefly described in the work *Late Babylonian Astronomical and Related Texts*, A. J. Sachs, ed. (Providence, R.I., 1955), no. 1419, p. xxxi, under "Descriptive Catalogue" as follows: "1419 . . . [a series of dates, -608/7 to "-446/5 . . ." including "-464/3" (465/64 B.C.)] Detailed reports of consecutive *lunar eclipses*, arranged in 18-year groups." The incidental mention of a date for the death of Xerxes is not included in this description but is given, on the authority of Sachs, by Parker and Dubberstein, *Babylonian Chronology, 626 B.C.-A.D. 75* (1956), p. 17. The date of Xerxes' murder is cited as 5th month, 14th-18th day (the day number is broken and therefore uncertain), 21st year (= August 4?-8?, 465 B.C.). Sachs' description was published 14 years ago, but the tablet is yet unpublished, and thus its contents are unavailable and its date and provenience are undisclosed; consequently the accuracy of its information cannot be evaluated. However, it is not necessary to await its publication in order to use it at least tentatively.

The last date, apparently, of a lunar eclipse mentioned on this tablet (-446/45, or 445/44 B.C.) gives no clue to how much later it may have been written, as long as it remains unpublished. However, it has been suggested that "the arrangement of the years on the various fragments indicates that nos. 1414-1417, 1419 belonged to a single large tablet that contained all the lunar eclipses of the years -739 to -308" (translated from Peter Huber, Review of Sachs' *Late Babylonian and Related Texts*, in *Bibliotheca Orientalis*, 13 [1956], p. 232). If that is true, the tablet in question was written more than 150 years after the death of Xerxes, in the Hellenistic period. The final verification of Huber's suggestion must await the publication of nos. 1414 and 1419 of *LBART*.

event mentioned. An evaluation of the text with regard to the time of its origin cannot be made until the tablet is published.

For this reason the information obtained from this tablet, hereafter referred to as *LBART 1419,* can be considered only as standing on the same level of reliability as other secondary sources from Hellenistic times mentioning Xerxes' death and Artaxerxes' accession to the throne. Such sources are available in considerable number. Unfortunately they are neither unanimous nor reliable, as the following discussion will show.

Earliest record from a Greek historian.—The earliest extant account of the murder of Xerxes—earlier than the Hellenistic period—comes from Ctesias, a Greek physician at the court of Artaxerxes II, who came to the throne only 60 years after Xerxes' death. Ctesias lived in Persia, knew the Persian language, and apparently had access to the Persian archives and to the story as told by the royal family. Unfortunately his historical work *Persica* is extant only in a summary made by Photius of the 9th century A.D.

Ctesias relates that King Xerxes was assassinated by Artabanus, a powerful courtier, with the help of a palace chamberlain. Artabanus then convinced the king's younger son, Artaxerxes, that his older brother Darius had committed this crime, and thus obtained permission from Artaxerxes to put Darius to death. Thereupon Artaxerxes, backed by Artabanus, became king. Later, when Artabanus decided to remove the young king and seize the throne for himself, he sought the help of Megabyzus, Artaxerxes' brother-in-law, but Megabyzus revealed not only this plot to the king but also the facts about the murders of Xerxes and Darius. Thereupon Artabanus was put to death. In the ensuing war against the partisans of Artabanus, three of his sons were killed.[29]

Ctesias probably reflects the official version as told from Artaxerxes' point of view. Unfortunately he does not say how long Artabanus remained in control or how he met his death. Yet his original account possibly contained further details, now lost, that may have been drawn on by subsequent writers.

Later historians.—Later ancient writers furnish other details (see Appendix 4 for source data), not all agreeing but not presenting great or glaring discrepancies, which permit us to obtain a fairly good picture of how the murder of Xerxes gave Artabanus temporary control of the kingdom and how he nearly succeeded in killing Artaxerxes before the young king was able to assert himself and establish his rule.

Diodorus of Sicily (late 1st century B.C.), who places Xerxes' death in 465/64 B.C., gives the impression that the whole upheaval required very little time, that Artabanus soon attacked the new king and was killed by his intended victim; yet he says that it took Artaxerxes two years to settle his kingdom.[30]

On the other hand, Trogus Pompeius [31] (1st century

---

[29] Ctesias *Persica* (Summary by Photius) 29, 30. For this narrative, see below, Appendix 4, pp. 160, 161.
[30] See pp. 161-163.   [31] See pp. 163, 164.

104

B.C. to 1st century A.D.), like Ctesias, implies an interval between Artabanus' murder of Xerxes and his plot against Artaxerxes, during which Artabanus let the latter occupy the throne, at least in name, and he himself retained his office as a courtier, powerful but still fearing a struggle among the nobles. Then the king, "only a boy," hearing of the plot, called a review of the troops, where he tricked Artabanus into disarming himself and killed him. Even after that, Artaxerxes had to struggle for some time against the partisans of Artabanus before he was in full control of the throne.

Artabanus is never described as "king" by the extant ancient historians. They refer to Artaxerxes as "king," but to Artabanus as "powerful" (Ctesias),[32] "captain of the royal bodyguard" (Diodorus),[33] "chief officer" (Trogus),[34] "satrap" (Nepos),[35] and "the chiliarch" ("commander of a thousand men"), who apparently controlled personal access to Artaxerxes when the exiled Greek general Themistocles sought refuge with the king of Persia (Plutarch).[36] Only one ancient king list, in the epitome of a history of Manetho, an Egyptian priest (3d century B.C.), lists Artabanus as one of the Persian *kings* of Egypt with a reign of 7 months between Xerxes and Artaxerxes.[37] Manetho was

---

[32] See p. 160.
[33] See p. 161.
[34] See p. 163.
[35] See p. 164.
[36] See p. 165. The disagreement among ancient writers as to whether Themistocles saw Xerxes or Artaxerxes would be accounted for if he arrived at the time of transition. He may have originally sought an audience with Xerxes but arrived just at the time of the assassination, or soon after, and so had to deal with Artabanus and Artaxerxes—possibly even before it became generally known that Xerxes was dead.
[37] See p. 166.

followed by the Christian chronographers Africanus (3d century A.D.) and Eusebius (4th century A.D.).[38] It is quite possible that the ascendancy of Artabanus lasted seven months (assigned to Artabanus by Manetho), or even longer. In any event, there was a period during which the young Artaxerxes was either a puppet king under the *de facto* rule of the powerful Artabanus or a contender in a struggle for control of the kingdom. This picture emerges clearly from the combined historical accounts, which with a few differences in detail agree on the principal facts.[39]

There are no known documents from any part of the Persian empire recognizing a reign of Artabanus. Unfortunately this negative evidence is weak, because there are no known contemporary records dated in either the last year of Xerxes or the accession year of Artaxerxes, except the Aramaic papyrus *AP 6*. It is

---

[38] See p. 167.

[39] There are two discrepant statements, both incidental remarks, which differ from all the others:

(1) Aristotle (4th century B.C.) says that Artabanus had already hanged Darius, the older son, before he murdered Xerxes (see p. 161). This mere incidental allusion, if not an error, may represent a variant rumor.

(2) Aelian (3d century A.D.) says that the killer was Xerxes' son (see p. 166). This brief remark, which agrees with no other Greek source, may reflect a tradition handed down by the partisans of Artabanus.

Such a tradition, if true (that is, if Artabanus had been falsely accused of Darius' crime, either by the informer Megabyzus or by Artaxerxes himself), would not essentially alter the picture presented by the other accounts of the power struggle between Artaxerxes and Artabanus. With Xerxes murdered, and Darius executed—whether deservedly or on a false accusation—the powerful Artabanus could take the reins in his own hands, at least as long as the other son, Hystaspes, was absent and Artaxerxes, a mere boy, could be used as a convenient puppet. This uneasy and uncertain situation would have lasted until the young Artaxerxes moved to end an intolerable menace to his crown, and perhaps his life, by outwitting and killing Artabanus. Afterward the most obvious method of justifying himself (and exonerating his brother Darius) would be to name Artabanus as the assassin and usurper who had caused the whole upheaval in order to gain the throne for himself. Then Artaxerxes' story—whether false or true—would naturally have gone into the official archives, and thus would have prevailed among later historians.

among the ironies of history that, although many thousands of dated documents of the Persian empire period survive, the year 465/4 is one of the poorest years represented.

In papyrus *AP 6* the double regnal date "year 21, . . . accession year" may reflect the uncertainty experienced by scribes in writing legal documents; they had heard that Xerxes was no longer alive and that Artaxerxes was probably the new king, but were not certain that this situation was final, since news of Artabanus' power may also have reached their ears. Such a period of unrest and confusion would explain an artificial extension of Xerxes' regnal numbering after his death, as attested by that papyrus. This will be discussed in subsequent sections.

Modern interpretations of the date.—Before archeologists brought to light contemporary documents of the Persian empire period the chronology of the Persian kings was based entirely on Ptolemy's Canon[40] and on statements of the ancient Greek historians. The regnal years of Artaxerxes I, for example, have been frequently the subject of discussion during the past three centuries, especially among Biblical historians who endeavored to date his 7th and 20th years, which are mentioned in the Bible. (Ussher, for example, dated the events of Ezra 7, in the 7th year, in 467 B.C.; Scaliger placed them in 458, and Isaac Newton in 457.)[41]

Modern historians have usually derived a composite picture of Artaxerxes' accession from the combined ac-

---

counts of the Greek historians. W. W. Tarn, apparently accepting the testimony of the Manetho king list, says that Artabanus reigned seven months and was recognized in Egypt,[42] but most writers on that period ignore Artabanus altogether for lack of tangible evidence that he played any decisive role before Artaxerxes' accession to the throne.

Ancient texts throw light on a troubled period.— It is now time to return to the ancient texts which date Xerxes' death and the accession of Artaxerxes. Unfortunately only two such texts exist; and one of them (the tablet *LBART 1419*) is not a contemporary document,[43] while the other (the double-dated Aramaic papyrus *AP 6*) poses a problem of interpretation because it is dated in the reign of two kings, one of whom was already dead.[44]

It is fortunate for our understanding of this papyrus that other examples of this same unusual type of year formula—extending the regnal numbering of a king after his death—have been found on ancient contemporary documents. Three cuneiform tablets—each, like *AP 6,* dated in two reigns (i.e. of Artaxerxes I and Darius II)—come from a transition period which was likewise filled with plots and counterplots, assassinations and power upsets, when Artaxerxes I was succeeded within a few months by Xerxes II, Secydianus (Sogdianus), and finally Darius II.[45] These tablets seem to indicate that the scribes who wrote them were un-

---

42 See p. 170.
43 See pp. 102, 103.
44 See pp. 100-102, 109-115.
45 See pp. 170, 171.

108

willing to stop dating by Artaxerxes' reign as long as there was uncertainty whether Darius would remain on the throne.

Another such exceptional situation in dating is found earlier, in the transitional period from Kandalanu to Nabopolassar in Babylon, where two tablets are dated in Kandalanu's name even in the year after his death.[46] This period also was one of political upheaval, when Assyria lost its control over Babylonia with the revolt of Nabopolassar.

It is significant that all these tablets, as well as papyrus *AP 6*, which exhibit these unusual year dates, were written in periods when an uncertain political situation provided a reason to extend a reign artificially into the period of a new king's accession year, indicating doubt as to the permanency of the new reign.

Papyrus AP 6 examined.—We have thus seen that a king's reign was in certain cases, both before and after *AP 6* was written, extended artificially beyond his death. This means that the double dating of *AP 6* in the reigns of both Xerxes and Artaxerxes is not necessarily a scribal error, nor is it necessarily a date in two calendars (since these other unusual documents are dated in only one calendar). However, in exploring all the possibilities, it is necessary to examine the date line of *AP 6* with the two-calendar alternative in mind, and ask: Are the two year dates expressed in two calendars, Egyptian and Semitic? Or in only one calendar? And if so, which one, the Egyptian or the Semitic?

---

[46] See pp. 171, 172.

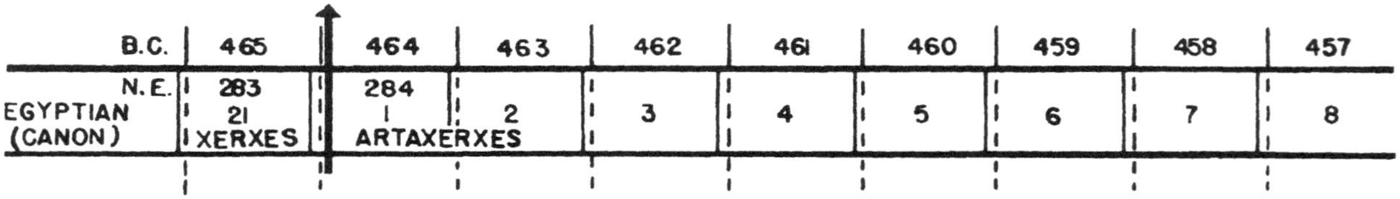

B.C.	465	464	463	462	461	460	459	458	457
N.E.	283	284							
EGYPTIAN (CANON)	21 XERXES	1 ARTAXERXES	2	3	4	5	6	7	8

Figure 5. ARTAXERXES IN THE EGYPTIAN CALENDAR

The last regnal year (21) of Xerxes and the early years of Artaxerxes are shown here as reckoned in the Egyptian calendar, compared with the B.C. scale. The Egyptian years, beginning in December in this period, run a little earlier than the B.C. years (shown extended by broken lines). The N.E. (Nabonassar era) numbering, derived from Ptolemy's Canon, is indicated for B.C. 466/65 and 465/64. The arrow shows the date of the papyrus *AP 6* (Jan. 2/3, 464 B.C.).

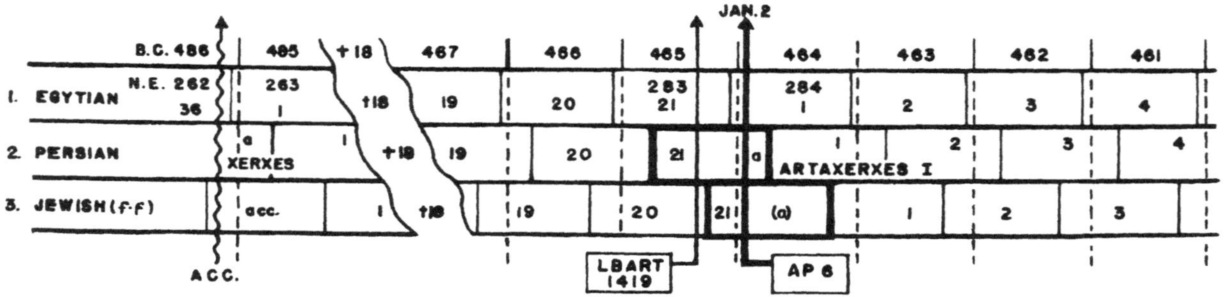

Figure 6. XERXES AND ARTAXERXES IN THREE CALENDARS

The regnal years of Xerxes (shortened in this drawing by an 18-year gap) and the early years of Artaxerxes are shown as reckoned (1) in the Egyptian calendar, with years beginning in December; (2) in the Persian calendar, with years beginning in the spring; and (3) in the Jewish calendar, with years beginning in the autumn; all three aligned against the background of the B.C. years (extended by broken lines). The three vertical arrows represent, from left to right, (1) the accession of Xerxes, some time in November, 486 B.C.; (2) the death of Xerxes (August 4-8, 465 B.C., if the tablet *LBART* no. 1419 is correct); and (3) the date of the papyrus *AP 6*, Jan. 2/3, 464 B.C.

No Egyptian year date.—First, if the date line of *AP 6* represents the year in the two calendars in which the month dates (Kislev 18 and Thoth [17]) are expressed, then either the "year 21" of Xerxes or the "accession year of Artaxerxes" must have been reckoned in the Egyptian calendar. However, this is not the case, as Figure 5 will demonstrate, in which the heavy arrow represents the date given in the papyrus, Jan. 2/3, 464 B.C. This arrow falls neither in the year 21 of Xerxes nor in the accession year of Artaxerxes in the Egyptian calendar, because year 21 had already ended and year 1 had already begun in December, as proved by Ptolemy's astronomically fixed Canon and by double dated papyri in both reigns.[47]

Even Manetho's seven-month reign of Artabanus could not account for this, for there would be less than five months from August (Xerxes' death date according to the Hellenistic tablet) and the January date of papyrus *AP 6*.

Therefore, since "year 21" and "accession year" in *AP 6* cannot be Egyptian dates, they must be Semitic—either the Babylonian-Persian year beginning with Nisan, in spring, or the Jewish year beginning with Tishri, in the fall.

Persian reckoning of the transition year.—How the double reckoning of *AP 6* works out in the Persian calendar is demonstrated in Figure 6, which shows the Egyptian, Persian, and Jewish reckoning of the regnal years. The Persian years are shown in the second band;

---

[47] See pp. 172-174.

and the Persian year 465/64 B.C., in which Xerxes died and Artaxerxes I came to the throne, is encased by heavy lines. The thin vertical arrow is the August death date according to the Hellenistic tablet *LBART 1419;* the heavy arrow is the date of the contemporary papyrus *AP 6,* in January. If the information on the Hellenistic tablet is correct, it was five months after Xerxes' death that the scribe of papyrus *AP 6* was still dating in Xerxes' year 21, though he conveyed the information that a new king was—at least temporarily— on the throne by adding the "accession year" of Artaxerxes (which in the Persian calendar would change on the following Nisanu 1, April 13, 464, to "year 1").[48]

Since there are extant parallel examples of double-dated documents from other times when a political upheaval after a king's death caused uncertainties with regard to the monarch who eventually would occupy the throne (in the time of the change from Kandalanu to Nabopolassar, and from Artaxerxes I to Darius II, as already shown), there is no reason to doubt that the double year date on *AP 6* was the result of the scribe's uncertainty as to whether Artabanus, Artaxerxes, or possibly his brother Hystaspes would eventually emerge as the permanent king, though Artaxerxes was already at least the titular king, as attested by the mention of his name. It cannot, then, be ruled out that the double-year dating of *AP 6* may have been made according to the Persian calendar, though the Jewish is more likely.

---

[48] See the Parker-Dubberstein tables for the date.

Jewish reckoning of the accession.—The papyrus *AP 6* is part of an archive of documents dealing with the affairs of a *Jewish* military colony, whose members had lived at Elephantine long before the Persians took over Egypt under Cambyses. It is reasonable to assume that they had clung to their own calendar system and had not adopted the Persian calendar—the more so since they had not taken over the Egyptian calendar, else they would not have needed double dating. It seems most likely that they still employed their ancient Hebrew calendar, in use at least from the time of Solomon—a calendar which began each year with Tishri, the 7th month, and which was employed in the reckoning of the years of their own former kings and of foreign rulers. *AP 6*, which dealt with an agreement over a disputed piece of land between a Jew and another man who, to judge by his name, may have been a Persian, was written by a Jewish scribe, and most of the witnesses were Jews.[49] It is therefore reasonable to assume that the Jewish calendar was used.

If this was the case, how would the events of the year 465/64 have affected the dating of documents? See the 3d band on Figure 6, where the Jewish year 465/64 is encased in heavy lines. Assuming again that the Hellenistic tablet is correct in dating Xerxes' death in August, 465, Jewish scribes after hearing of his death would then have dated any documents in the accession year of his successor, either Artabanus or

---

[49] See Cowley, *op. cit.*, pp. 15-18, where a transliteration and translation of *AP 6* with some linguistic notes on the document are given.

Artaxerxes. If it was Artaxerxes, then on their New Year's Day, on Tishri 1 (Oct. 18), 465,[50] they would normally have switched to year 1 of Artaxerxes. But *AP 6*, written in January, 464, is still dated in the *accession* year of Artaxerxes, which indicates that they had not recognized Artaxerxes on the throne before Tishri, either because Artabanus was at that time recognized as the *de facto* king, or because the political upheaval in Persia made it simply impossible to know who would emerge from the struggle as the permanent king. Consequently the 21st regnal year of Xerxes was continued in legal documents as long as the uncertainty remained as to who eventually would be king. When the news was received that Artaxerxes was on the throne, but no full certainty about his permanency was ascertainable because of the continuing power struggle, the information that it was Artaxerxes' accession year was added in the date line to the 21st year of his dead father. The very fact that in January, 464, a Jewish scribe dated a document in the "accession year of Artaxerxes" shows that, as far as the evidence was available to this Jewish scribe, Artaxerxes had not come to the throne before Tishri 1. For this reason his year 1 would not begin until Tishri 1, 464. On the other hand, it should not be forgotten that the August date for Xerxes' death is based on a non-historical text (*LBART 1419*) apparently written at least 130 years

---

[50] The equivalents of the Jewish dates are taken from the Horn-Wood reconstruction of the Jewish calendar based on the dated Elephantine papyri. See for this calendar Appendix 3, pp. 157-159. The dates are approximately the same as those of Parker and Dubberstein.

after the event had occurred, for which no independent evidence exists to prove its accuracy. Because of this uncertainty it is a possibility that Xerxes' death occurred after Tishri 1, 465, but certainly by Jan. 2, 464, as attested by *AP 6*.

This evidence makes it certain that the Jewish scribe, Nehemiah, who used a civil fall-to-fall calendar, would begin to reckon the first regnal year of Artaxerxes on Tishri 1, 464 B.C., and not in 465.

Ezra's journey in the seventh year of Artaxerxes.— Consequently, if the 1st year of Artaxerxes I ran from the fall of 464 to the fall of 463 B.C. according to Jewish reckoning, the king's 7th year ran from the fall of 458 to the fall of 457 B.C., as is clear in Figure 7 (page 116). Then Ezra's journey, which began on Nisan 1 and ended on Ab 1 of the 7th year of Artaxerxes (Ezra 7:8, 9), reached from late March to late July, 457 B.C.

The evidence presented in chapter 4, not only from Nehemiah but also from an Elephantine papyrus (*Kraeling 6*), shows that the Jews reckoned a Persian king's years according to a fall-to-fall year. In the present chapter it is established that Artaxerxes' accession year extended into 464 B.C.—long after Tishri 1, 465— and hence his year 1 was 464/63 B.C. This places the dates given in the preceding paragraph on a sound basis. These documents, taken together with the Biblical statements of Nehemiah and Ezra, lead to the inescapable conclusion that the decree of Artaxerxes I went into effect, after Ezra's return from Babylon, in the late summer or early fall of 457 B.C.

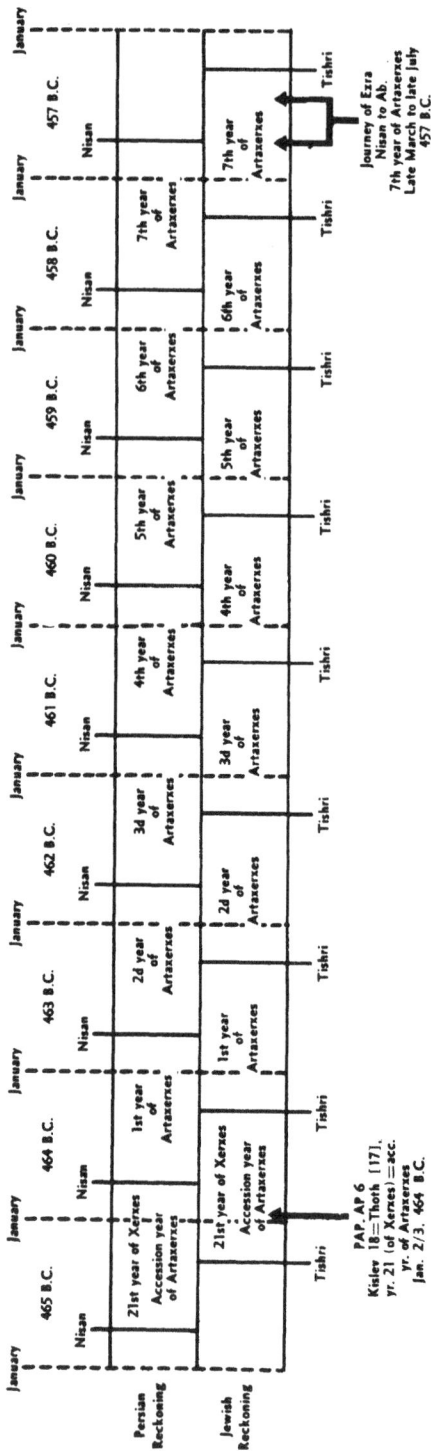

Fig. 7

From the Twenty-first Year of Xerxes to the Seventh Year of Artaxerxes I

This chart shows that the end of the accession year of Artaxerxes in 464 B.C. caused the first regnal year of Artaxerxes, according to Jewish reckoning, to begin in the fall of that same year. Hence the journey of Ezra in the seventh Jewish year of Artaxerxes occurred entirely in 457 B.C.

CHAPTER SIX

Summary of the Findings

THE CAREFUL reader of the preceding chapters will have gained an idea of the vast problems connected with the dating of historical events of antiquity. He has thus become acquainted with different calendars, and with varying methods of counting calendar years or regnal years of kings in use among ancient nations.

The counting of regnal years.—The historical evidence indicates that the different nations had various methods of reckoning the regnal years of their kings by calendar years.[1] The Egyptians used a method in which the death year of one king became also the first one of his successor, called the non-accession-year (or antedating) system. However, the peoples of the Mesopotamian valley used a method called the accession-year (or postdating) system, since they designated the unexpired portion of the death year of one king as his successor's accession year, and began the new king's year 1 only on the following New Year's Day. Under the divided kingdoms of Israel and Judah both systems were used at different times, depending on whether

---

[1] See pp. 15-22.

Egypt, Assyria, or Babylonia had greater influence on the two small nations in Palestine.

Solar and lunar calendars.—Owing to the fact that a solar year is divisible neither by full lunar months nor by whole days, different systems of reckoning years were used.

The Egyptians employed a solar year of 365 days.[2] Since this was about one-quarter of a day short of a true solar year, their New Year's Day moved backward in relation to the seasons one day every four years, thus wandering through all the seasons in the course of 1,460 years. However, the difference in one lifetime was not great, and throughout the 5th century B.C., with which this study is concerned, the Egyptian New Year's Day fell in December. From the Egyptian solar calendar was derived the Julian calendar, still in use today, with slight modifications, under the name of the Gregorian calendar.

The Mesopotamian peoples, on the other hand, developed a luni-solar year[3] by which the months were regulated by length of the moon's rotation around the earth, and in which 12 lunar months, varying between 29 and 30 days, made up an ordinary year. Since such years were 10 to 11 days shorter than a solar year, in every 2d or 3d year an extra month was inserted in the middle or at the end to bring the calendar year in harmony with the seasons. The New Year's Day was celebrated on Nisan 1, in the spring, and fell in March

---

[2] See pp. 34-45.
[3] See pp. 35, 36, 45-48.

or April. The Persian rulers adopted this calendar system when they gained possession of the Babylonian empire.

The Biblical evidence shows that the Jews had a luni-solar year like the other nations of Western Asia,[4] but their intercalary months were apparently inserted only between the 12th and 1st lunar months in the spring, not between the 6th and 7th also, as was frequently done in Mesopotamia. The Bible shows us, furthermore, that the Jews employed two calendar years, one—introduced by Moses—for religious purposes, which like the Babylonian calendar began with Nisan in the spring, and another one for civil and agricultural purposes, beginning with the first of Tishri in the fall. The numbering of the months, however, was always begun with Nisan; for example, the number "seven" was employed for Tishri, whether that month was referred to as part of the ecclesiastical or the civil year.[5]

Systems used to count Persian regnal years.—During the period of the Persian Empire, when one king ruled over many formerly independent nations, dating throughout the empire was done according to the regnal years of Persian kings. However, the subject peoples retained their own systems of reckoning such regnal years.

The evidence of Ptolemy's Canon[6]—known for a

---

[4] See chapter 3.
[5] See p. 74.
[6] See pp. 40-43.

long time—seemed to indicate that the years of the Persian kings were reckoned in Egypt according to the Egyptian calendar. The Elephantine papyri have provided contemporary source material showing that this was so. They also show that the Egyptians evidently did not use the accession-year system, as did the Babylonians and Persians, but counted the regnal years of Persian kings as they had formerly done with their own kings, using the non-accession-year system (with possible exceptions; see p. 173, note 30). It is also evident that they began each regnal year with their own New Year's Day, which fell four to five months before the Persian one in the 5th century B.C.,[7] so that there was only a partial overlapping between the regnal years as reckoned by the Egyptian and Persian systems. Several papyri show that in any date falling between the Egyptian and Persian New Year's Days, the Egyptian regnal-year number was always higher than the Persian.

The Biblical evidence shows that the Jews had used the accession-year system in the Babylonian period, so that it could be assumed that they retained this method after the Exile in common with Persian practice. This conclusion has been proved correct by the contemporary Jewish documents from Elephantine.[8]

The Bible also indicates, through the information given by Nehemiah, that the Jews in Palestine counted the years of Artaxerxes I according to their own civil

---

[7] See pp. 79-81.
[8] The fact that the Jewish year runs later than the Persian in *AP 25* and *28* shows that the Jews used an accession year before the 1st year.

calendar, which began in the fall (Tishri). Those who have accepted Nehemiah's statements as reliable source material have held that his method of dating the regnal years of a Persian king according to a fall-to-fall calendar was not due to his idiosyncrasy but was a common practice among the Jews, which can be traced back from Nehemiah's time to the reign of King Solomon.

From these indications the conclusion can be reached that the years of Artaxerxes I were counted by Ezra and Nehemiah according to their own system, so that each of his regnal years was the same according to the Persian and Jewish systems of reckoning during one half year but differed during the other half year.

Two key problems.—The establishment of the correct dates for the events described in Ezra 7, with which this study is concerned, hinges on two key problems. The first one is to determine whether the Jews of Nehemiah's time actually reckoned the years of the Persian kings according to their own civil fall-to-fall calendar. The second problem is to find the exact time of Artaxerxes' accession, in order to determine whether the regnal years in the Jewish fall-to-fall reckoning ran earlier or later than the corresponding Persian years.

Evidence for the Jewish fall-to-fall calendar.—The first problem existed since the reliability of Nehemiah's statements has been challenged, and it was thought by many scholars that scribal errors might be involved in his figures. It was therefore desirable to obtain extra-Biblical dated Jewish documents to give us more information about the Jewish calendars. Although hundreds

121

of thousands of dated cuneiform tablets are available for the establishment of the Babylonian calendar, which was used also by the Persians, and hundreds of documents inform us about the ancient Egyptian calendar, only a few well-preserved Jewish documents of the 5th century B.C. were available until very recent times for the Jewish calendar.

The recent discovery, in the Brooklyn Museum, of 8 fairly well-preserved, dated Aramaic papyri of the same period has increased to 14 the number of double-dated documents available for a reconstruction of the Jewish calendar. Though this is still a small number in comparison with the wealth of material that sheds light on the Egyptian and Babylonian calendars, these papyri are nevertheless of great importance for the study of the chronology of Ezra, since they all come from the same period.[9]

Although all of these 14 documents bear double dates—Jewish and Egyptian—ten of them mention the year number of the Persian king only according to the Egyptian reckoning—apparently the customary legal requirement in Egypt, where the writers of these documents lived. They naturally do not throw any light on the Jewish calendar. Two papyri contain the Jewish as well as Egyptian year numbers, showing a difference of one year between them in each case. Unfortunately, both of them come from a portion of the year in which there was no difference between the year numbers in

---

[9] For the Aramaic papyri and their bearing on the Jewish fall-to-fall reckoning, see pp. 75-90.

the Persian and Jewish systems of reckoning, and the difference between the Egyptian and Persian systems of reckoning was equal to the difference between the Egyptian and Jewish systems.

Two papyri contain the regnal year number of the Persian king according to the Jewish system of reckoning, but one of them again comes from that portion of the year when there is no difference between the Persian and Jewish way of reckoning regnal years, so that this papyrus contains once more no proof for a different method used by the Jews. One of the newly discovered papyri, however, which contains only the regnal year of the Persian king according to the Jewish way of reckoning (*Kraeling 6*),[10] comes from that half year which lies between Nisan and Tishri, when there was a difference between the Persian and Jewish regnal numbering. Hence, it shows clearly that the Jews used a fall-to-fall calendar in their reckoning of regnal years of Persian kings, as Figure 4 illustrates.[11]

The only other explanation for this papyrus would be the assumption of a scribal error, an explanation that has also been used by higher critics for the statements of Nehemiah that point to a fall-to-fall calendar of the Jews. Since the new papyrus, however, forms an independent support for Nehemiah's practice, there is no reason to assume the existence of scribal errors in either case—the book of Nehemiah or the Elephantine document. The new evidence thus shows clearly

---

[10] See pp. 84-88.
[11] See p. 86.

that the Jews in Elephantine used a fall-to-fall calendar as their contemporaries in Judah did.

The publication, in 1956, of a newly discovered Babylonian Chronicle of Nebuchadnezzar's time brought to light some additional evidence for the existence of the Jewish fall-to-fall calendar, and for the fact that the regnal years of foreign kings were reckoned according to this Jewish calendar.[12] In conclusion it can thus be said that the Biblical data, supported by the Babylonian Chronicle for the pre-exilic period and by the Elephantine papyri for the postexilic period, make the existence and use of the civil fall-to-fall calendar among Jews quite certain.

The accession of Artaxerxes determined.—The solution of the second problem is needed in order to determine whether this regnal year of Artaxerxes I according to Jewish reckoning preceded or followed that of the Persians.[13] If he began to reign between Nisan and Tishri, the following Jewish New Year would come before the Persian New Year; hence Jewish years would run 6 months ahead of the Persian years, for the Jews, beginning the first year of the king in Tishri, counted it as such while it was still the accession year for the Persians until the next spring. If he came to the throne between Tishri and Nisan, the Persian year 1 would begin first in Nisan, but the Jews would continue to count that regnal year as the accession year until the next Tishri, 6 months later than the Persian year.

---

[12] See pp. 64-67.
[13] See chapter 5.

SUMMARY OF THE FINDINGS

If the exact time of accession of a king is not ascertainable, an uncertainty remains as to which Jewish year is the accession year and which the 1st year, and the conversion of a Jewish date into the Julian calendar may be off by one year. For Artaxerxes I this uncertainty still exists to a certain degree. The only document dated in the calendar year in which Xerxes' death and Artaxerxes' accession occurred gives us merely the information that Artaxerxes had come to the throne before Jan. 2, 464 B.C. However, this document is one of the Jewish Elephantine papyri, and therefore applies the Jewish fall-to-fall calendar in its date line. It must be remembered that this document, written between Tishri, 465, and Nisan, 464, is dated "accession year of Artaxerxes." This shows that Artaxerxes could not have come to the throne, or at least was not recognized in Elephantine as king, until after Tishri 1. Otherwise the Jewish scribe would have written "year 1 of Artaxerxes" and not accession year. In this same document the equating of Artaxerxes' accession year with the 21st year of Xerxes—although Xerxes may have died in August, according to an unconfirmed report of a Hellenistic scribe—reflects an uncertainty caused by a power struggle after Xerxes' murder. This explains why the scribe continued to use the slain Xerxes' year 21 until it was certain which contender would hold the throne. Examples from other periods, before and after Artaxerxes' reign, prove this reasoning correct.[14]

Therefore we can conclude with reasonable cer-

---

[14] See pp. 170-172.

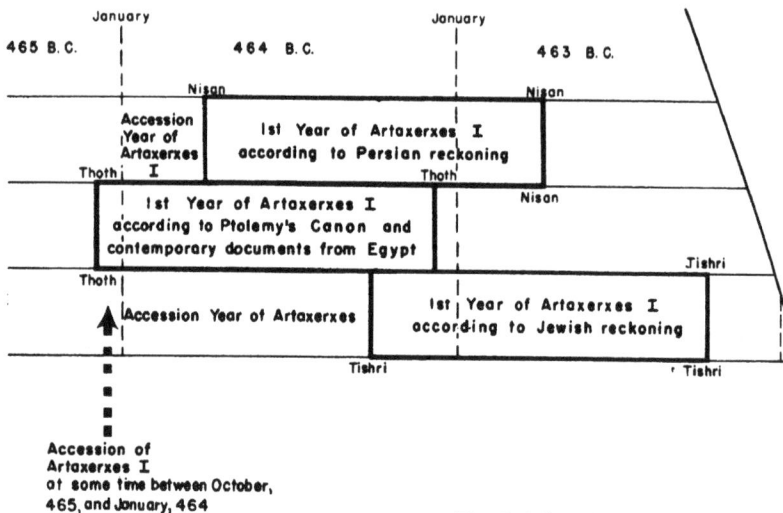

Fig. 8. The First and Seventh

The relationship of the Persian, Egyptian, and Jewish calendar
years of Artaxerxes, indicating how it came

tainty that Artaxerxes was not recognized as coming to
the throne before Tishri 1 (Oct. 18), 465 B.C. The
Jews thus counted the months following his accession
to the throne until the fall of 464 as his accession year,
and his regnal years began, according to Jewish reckoning, always 6 months later than according to the Persian
count. (Figure 8.)

Artaxerxes' decree effective in 457 B.C.—The solution of the two problems by recent archeological material has based the dating of the events described in
Ezra 7 on a sure foundation. The Aramaic papyrus
Kraeling 6, written by Jews in Elephantine, shows that
the Jews there used a fall-to-fall calendar for reckoning
the regnal years of a Persian king, and the Elephantine
papyrus *AP 6* proves that Artaxerxes was not unequiv-
ocally recognized as king before Tishri 1, 465 B.C.,
his father's reign being extended artificially into 464.

126

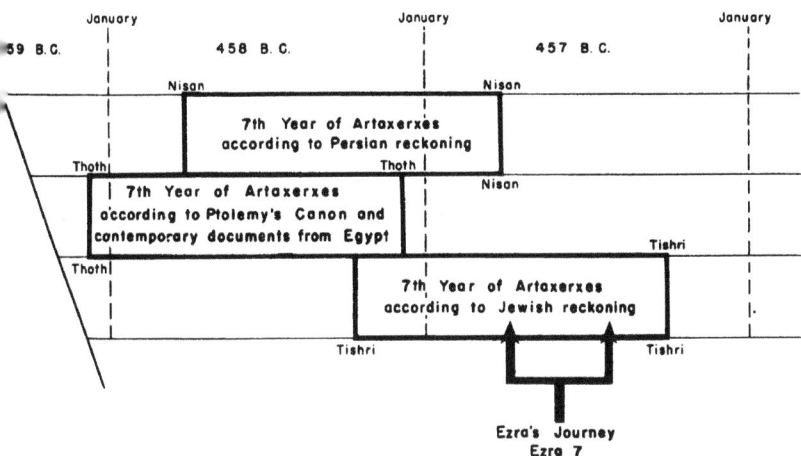

January ··· 59 B.C. ··· 458 B.C. ··· January ··· 457 B.C. ··· January

Nisan ··· Nisan

7th Year of Artaxerxes
according to Persian reckoning

Thoth ··· Thoth ··· Nisan

7th Year of Artaxerxes
according to Ptolemy's Canon and
contemporary documents from Egypt

Tishri

Thoth

7th Year of Artaxerxes
according to Jewish reckoning

Tishri ··· Tishri

Ezra's Journey
Ezra 7

Years of Artaxerxes I

years to the Julian calendar is shown for the first and seventh
that Ezra's journey took place in 457 B.C.

Consequently, Jews who used a fall-to-fall calendar
for expressing the regnal years of Artaxerxes I began
the counting of his first year in the fall of 464 B.C. and
ended that first year in the fall of 463 B.C., as Figure 8
illustrates. According to this method the 7th year began
in the fall of 458 B.C. and ended in the fall of 457.

Since this method of reckoning the regnal years of
Persian kings can be shown to have been used by
Nehemiah in Palestine, and his compatriots in Egypt,
it is only reasonable to conclude that Ezra, Nehemiah's
predecessor and colaborer, did the same. In that case
Ezra's journey, which began in the month of Nisan of
the 7th year of Artaxerxes and ended in Ab (5th
month), took place from late March to late July in
457 B.C., and the decree of Artaxerxes I went into effect
after Ezra's arrival in Palestine in late summer or early
fall of that same year.

127

Appendix 1

PTOLEMY'S CANON OF THE KINGS

Of the Assyrians and Medes	Years	Totals	N.E.	Year Begins
Nabonassar	14	14	1	Feb. 26, 747 B.C.
Nadius	2	16	15	" 23, 733
Chinzer and Porus	5	21	17	" 22, 731
Iloulaius	5	26	22	" 21, 726
Mardokempad	12	38	27	" 20, 721
Arkean	5	43	39	" 17, 709
First Interregnum	2	45	44	" 15, 704
Bilib	3	48	46	" 15, 702
Aparanad	6	54	49	" 14, 699
Regebel	1	55	55	" 13, 693
Mesesimordak	4	59	56	" 12, 692
Second Interregnum	8	67	60	" 11, 688
Asaridin	13	80	68	" 9, 680
Saosdouchin	20	100	81	" 6, 667
Kinelanadan	22	122	101	" 1, 647
Nabopolassar	21	143	123	Jan. 27, 625
Nabokolassar [Nebuchadnezzar]	43	186	144	" 21, 604
Illoaroudam [Evil-Merodach]	2	188	187	" 11, 561
Nerigasolassar [Neriglissar]	4	192	189	" 10, 559
Nabonadius [Nabonidus]	17	209	193	" 9, 555
Of the Persian Kings				
Cyrus	9	218	210	" 5, 538
Cambyses	8	226	219	" 3, 529
Darius I	36	262	227	" 1, 521
Xerxes	21	283	263	Dec. 23, 486
Artaxerxes I	41	324	284	" 17, 465
Darius II	19	343	325	" 7, 424
Artaxerxes II	46	389	344	" 2, 405
Ochus	21	410	390	Nov. 21, 359
Arogus	2	412	411	" 16, 338
Darius III	4	416	413	" 15, 336
Alexander of Macedonia	8	424	417	" 14, 332
Of the Macedonian Kings	*Years*	*Totals*		
Philip	7	7	425	" 12, 324
Alexander II	12	19	432	" 10, 317
Ptolemy Lagus	20	39	444	" 7, 305
Philadelphus	38	77	464	" 2, 285
Euergetes I	25	102	502	Oct. 24, 247
Philopator	17	119	527	" 18, 222
Epiphanes	24	143	544	" 13, 205
Philometor	35	178	568	" 7, 181
Euergetes II	29	207	603	Sept. 29, 146
Soter	36	243	632	" 21, 117
Dionysius the Younger	29	272	668	" 12, 81
Cleopatra	22	294	697	" 5, 52
Of the Roman Kings				
Augustus	43	337	719	Aug. 31, 30 B.C.
Tiberius	22	359	762	" 20, 14 A.D.
Gaius	4	363	784	" 14, 36
Claudius	14	377	788	" 13, 40
Nero	14	391	802	" 10, 54
Vespasian	10	401	816	" 6, 68
Titus	3	404	826	" 4, 78
Domitian	15	419	829	" 3, 81
Nerva	1	420	844	July 30, 96
Trajan	19	439	845	" 30, 97
Hadrian	21	460	864	" 25, 116
Aelius-Antonine [Antoninus Pius]	23	483	885	" 20, 137

Yr. 1 of Each Reign by Egyptian Calendar

Appendix 2

THE FIFTH-CENTURY JEWISH CALENDAR
AT ELEPHANTINE [1]

The only 5th-century documents shedding light on the calendar of the Jews during the time of Ezra and Nehemiah are the Aramaic papyri from Elephantine and one stone monument in the Cairo Museum. The papyri, numbering more than 100, throw welcome light on the language, history, and everyday life of a Jewish garrison town in Egypt; and a number of these papyri form exceedingly important source material for the study of the calendar in use among the Jews during the 5th century B.C. Thirty-eight of the documents are dated, 22 of them bearing double dates—the Egyptian date and one which was used by the Jews, employing Babylonian month names. Since the Egyptian dates can easily be converted into those of the Julian calendar, means are thus provided for ascertaining the kind of calendar used by the Elephantine Jews.[2]

As soon as Sayce and Cowley published the first group of papyri, several scholars attacked the problems involved

---

[1] This appendix appeared, essentially in the same form, as an article in *JNES*, 13 (1954), pp. 1-20.

[2] A synchronism between the known Egyptian calendar (see pp. 36-40) and variable lunar calendar (see pp. 45-48) makes it possible to date a double-dated papyrus correctly. If the Egyptian regnal-year number is known, the Egyptian month and day are sufficient to fix the B.C. date in the Julian calendar; but even if the exact location of the regnal year is uncertain, the double solar-lunar dating can determine the year as well as the month and day.

The reason for this can best be given by a concrete example. The regnal year 3 of Darius II in *Kraeling 6* (see Fig. 4, p. 86) might conceivably be either the Egyptian year 3, placing the document in 421 B.C., or the Jewish fall-to-fall regnal year 3, which would place the papyrus in 420 B.C. The Egyptian date alone does not determine which is correct, because Pharmuthi 8, moving back one day only every four years, is July 11/12 in both years. But the lunar date Tammuz 8 can agree with July 11/12 in only one of those years—in fact, only once in a number of years—since it shifts not less than 10 days from one year to the next. This illustrates the fact that any synchronism between solar- and lunar-calendar dates can occur in only one year within a range of several possible years (in this case, 420 B.C.), and the double date can thus locate a disputed regnal year independently of Ptolemy's Canon or the Saros Tablets.

in their dates and the calendar system used. E. Schürer[3] was one of the first who discussed the dates of these documents. He was followed by F. K. Ginzel.[4] Both of them started out from the hypothesis that the Jews of the 5th century had a lunar calendar like the Persians, and that they began every month after the visibility of the new moon as in Babylon. Irregularities and disagreements in the dates were explained as scribal mistakes. L. Belleli, however, tried to prove by the apparently inexplicable disagreements between some of the dates that the documents were modern forgeries,[5] but very few scholars could believe .that papyri found by a scientific expedition—as the majority of the papyri had come to light in this way— could have been dumped on the site by forgers who would have to profit from the discovery of the documents. Since the excavated papyri show the same characteristics as those bought from natives, no doubt in the genuineness of any of them can be reasonably entertained.

The astronomer E. B. Knobel showed from papyri *AP 13* and *25* that a 19-year cycle was known to the Jews in the 5th century B.C., as their system of intercalation shows. He concluded from his findings that the Jewish civil calendar was computed, and that the civil year began with Tishri 1.[6] The well-known British astronomer J. K. Fotheringham came similarly to the conclusion that the computed calendar and the year beginning with Tishri 1 were used, and

---

[3] Schürer, Book review: "Aramaic Papyri discovered at Assuan, edited by A. H. Sayce with the assistance of A. E. Cowley . . . London, A. Moring, 1906, . . ." *Theologische Literaturzeitung,* 32 (1907), cols. 1-7; also his "Der jüdische Kalender nach den aramäischen Papyri von Assuan. Nachtrag zu der Anzeige in Nr. 1," *ibid.,* cols. 65-69.

[4] Ginzel, *Handbuch der mathematischen und technischen Chronologie,* vol. 2, pp. 45-52.

[5] L. Belleli, *An Independent Examination of the Assuan and Elephantine Aramaic Papyri.*

[6] E. B. Knobel, "A Suggested Explanation of the Ancient Jewish Calendar Dates in the Aramaic Papyri Translated by Professor A. H. Sayce and Mr. A. E. Cowley," *Monthly Notices of the Royal Astronomical Society,* 68 (1907-1908), pp. 334-345; also his "Note on the Regnal Years in the Aramaic Papyri From Assuan," *ibid.,* 69 (1908-1909), pp. 8-11.

also that the intercalation was arbitrarily done by the insertion of a second Adar, not of a second Elul.[7] The chronologist E. Mahler agreed with Knobel and Fotheringham that the Jewish calendar was based neither on the visibility of the first crescent nor on the conjunction, but on the application of a regular cycle. However, he believed that the Jewish fall-to-fall calendar was a later institution.[8] Martin Sprengling, on the other hand, reached entirely different conclusions. Maintaining that the Jewish civil year, beginning with Tishri, was a later development, he held that the Elephantine papyri attest a year that began with Nisan, and that the Jews of the 5th century used a second Elul, but dropped it later on.[9] It is not necessary to review in detail the work of P. J. Hontheim, J.-B. Chabot, J. G. Smyly, D. Sidersky, and H. Pognon,[10] because their reasonings vary only in some details from the various conclusions reached by the scholars already mentioned. It should be stated, however, that S. Gutesmann thought the Jews possessed a 25-year cycle [11] instead of the Babylonian 19-year cycle. This theory has found no accept-

---

[7] J. K. Fotheringham, "Calendar Dates in the Aramaic Papyri from Assuan," *ibid.*, 69 (1908-1909), pp. 12-20; also his "Note on the Regnal Years in the Elephantine Papyri," *ibid.*, pp. 446-448; and his "A Reply to Professor Ginzel on the Calendar Dates in the Elephantine Papyri," *ibid.*, 71 (1911), pp. 661-663.

[8] Eduard Mahler, "Die Doppeldaten der aramäischen Papyri von Assuan," *Zeitschrift für Assyriologie*, 26 (1912), pp. 61-76; also his *Handbuch der jüdischen Chronologie*, pp. 346-360.

[9] Martin Sprengling, "Chronological Notes From the Aramaic Papyri, . . ." *AJSL*, 27 (1911), pp. 233-252.

[10] P. J. Hontheim, "Die neuentdeckten jüdisch-aramäischen Papyri von Assuan," *Biblische Zeitschrift*, 5 (1907), pp. 225-234; J.-B. Chabot, "Les papyri araméens d'Eléphantine sont-ils faux?" *Journal Asiatique*, 10th series, vol. 14 (1909), pp. 515-522; J. Gilbart Smyly, "An Examination of the Dates of the Assouan Aramaic Papyri," *Proceedings of the Royal Irish Academy*, vol. 27, sec. C (1908-1909), pp. 235-250; D. Sidersky, "Le calendrier sémitique des papyri araméens d'Assouan," *Journal Asiatique*, 10th series, vol. 16 (1910), pp. 587-592; H. Pognon, "Chronologie des papyrus araméens d'Eléphantine," *ibid.*, vol. 18 (1911), pp. 337-365.

[11] S. Gutesmann, "Sur le calendrier en usage chez les Israélites au Ve siècle avant notre ère," *Revue des études juives*, 53 (1907), p. 198. He said a cycle of 25 *Egyptian* 365-day years. The Egyptians had such a cycle—attested only later but undoubtedly representing an older method, says O. Neugebauer (*Exact Sciences in Antiquity*, pp. 90, 95)—in which their lunar festivals returned to the same Egyptian calendar dates every 25 years. But these did not concern the Jews.

131

ance, since the double-dated papyri would have to show more evidence for it than can be found in them. It seems unlikely that the Jews used it, for their festivals depended on the seasonal year, not on the shifting Egyptian year.

R. A. Parker, whose study seems to be the latest published on the Elephantine papyri, holds that they are dated in the Persian, i.e. Babylonian, calendar,[12] the divergences from the Egyptian dates being attributable to errors of scribes presumably unfamiliar with the Egyptian calendar and confused by double dating.[13]

The different views found in the numerous studies dealing with the dates of these papyri reveal that no unassailable conclusions have yet been reached. Most scholars, however, agree that a 19-year cycle was in use among the Jews of the 5th century B.C. Many also agree that the Jewish calendar was not completely synonymous with the Babylonian calendar, unless every divergence is explained as a scribal error.

With regard to other points there is much difference in opinion. Whether the Jews began their civil year with Nisan or Tishri, whether they made use of a second Elul besides the second Adar, and whether the intercalation was carried out regularly are disputed questions.

The great increase in the number of dated documents through the discovery of the Brooklyn Museum papyri makes a re-examination of the whole problem urgent. They are leading us a step further on the way to the final solution, as the following discussion will show. Although we are not yet able to explain every phase of the Jewish calendar method of the postexilic period, we actually know

---

[12] Richard A. Parker, "Persian and Egyptian Chronology," *AJSL*, 58 (1941), pp. 288-292.

[13] Parker, "Some Considerations on the Nature of the Fifth-Century Jewish Calendar at Elephantine," *JNES*, 14 (1955), pp. 271-274.

much more about it through these papyri than for the period of the first Christian century.

Procedures followed.—In the study of these papyri the first step will be to convert the Egyptian date into terms of the Julian calendar, which is a comparatively easy matter, as was shown in chapter 1, because of the invariable 365-day solar year used by the ancient Egyptians. The date arrived at in this way will cover parts of two Julian calendar days, since the Egyptian day began at dawn. Therefore, two figures will have to be used, and the formula July 7/8 (sr-sr),[14] 465 B.C., designates an Egyptian day that lasted from July 7 at dawn to July 8 at dawn in 465 B.C.

Since the Jews and Babylonians began the day at sunset, their day also overlaps two Julian calendar days, and Jewish dates will henceforth also be indicated by two figures. Thus July 7/8 (ss-ss),[15] 465 B.C., means the day which began at sunset July 7 and ended at sunset July 8. Thus the Egyptian day did not coincide exactly with the day as reckoned by any of the other peoples mentioned. Hence a legal document signed on the Egyptian day July 7/8 (sr-sr) would give two possible dates in terms of a Jewish calendar, depending on the part of the day when the signing of the document occurred. If it was signed before sunset, it would be dated to an earlier Jewish date than if it was signed after sunset.

If therefore a double-dated papyrus equates a certain Egyptian date with one of the Jewish calendar, it is still uncertain whether the Jewish day referred to began the evening preceding the Egyptian date mentioned, or on the evening of that Egyptian day. The Jews had a lunar

---

[14] It is generally held by scholars that the Egyptian day began at dawn. For practical purposes there is no difference between dawn and sunrise; hence the abbreviation "sr-sr" is used for sunrise to sunrise in contrast to the Jewish day, which lasted from sunset to sunset.

[15] The abbreviation "ss-ss" stands for sunset to sunset.

calendar, in which the first day of the month must begin a reasonable time after the conjunction (at least not much less than one day later). Our conclusions will therefore lead us in a few cases to assume that a document was made up after sunset,[16] if otherwise the time between conjunction and the beginning of the first day of the month at sunset would become too small to be reasonable. Thus it must be recognized that an uncertainty of one day cannot be avoided, because (1) the Egyptian and Jewish days did not completely overlap, and (2) the scribes in no case indicated the time of day when the document was written.

The Elephantine papyri were written for the most part in the time when Egypt was a Persian satrapy; therefore the dated papyri are with one exception (*AP 35*) dated according to regnal years of Persian kings. However, the Egyptian reckoning of the regnal year of a given Persian king began with Thoth 1, which during the 5th century B.C. fell about four months before Nisan, the first month of the Babylonian calendar, and about 10 months before Tishri, the first month of the Jewish civil calendar, as has been demonstrated.[17] Hence, any Egyptian document dated after Thoth 1, and before either the Persian or Jewish New Year's Day, had a regnal-year number which was higher by one than the corresponding Persian or Jewish year number.

It has already been shown that with very few exceptions the regnal-year numbers are given according to the Egyptian system of reckoning such years. This seems to have been ordinarily required in Egypt for all legal documents, such as the double-dated papyri.[18]

---

[16] For "sunset" a mean is taken, for the purposes of this study, at 6 P.M. Elephantine civil time (that is, local time at Elephantine, counted from midnight), although this time naturally varied somewhat during the seasons of the year.

[17] See pp. 79, 80 and Fig. 3, for the Persian system, and pp. 84-87 and Fig. 4 for the Jewish in relation to the Egyptian.

[18] See pp. 81, 82.

JEWISH CALENDAR AT ELEPHANTINE

After having briefly explained the procedures followed in the interpretation of the double dates, we shall proceed to their discussion, taking them up in chronological sequence. The reader who has carefully read chapters 1 and 2 should find no difficulty in understanding the following discussion.

AP 5. Elul 18 =·Pachons 28, year 15 of Xerxes (471 B.C.)

The 15th year of Xerxes is the year 277 of the Nabonassar era of Ptolemy's Canon beginning Dec. 19, 472 B.C., and lasting through Dec. 18, 471 B.C. Pachons 28 fell on Sept. 12/13 (sr-sr), 471 B.C. Since the Jewish day began at sunset, as has already been explained, Elul 18 would not coincide exactly with Pachons 28, but would overlap parts of two Egyptian days. Therefore (see Fig. 9, p. 136) there are two possibilities: (1) Sept. 11/12 (ss-ss) if the agreement was drawn up during the hours of the day, or (2) Sept. 12/13 (ss-ss) if it was written after sunset of Sept. 12. This would then result in two possible dates for Elul 1 (see Fig. 10, p. 138), either (1) Aug. 25/26 (ss-ss) if the document was written during the hours of the day, or (2) Aug. 26/27 (ss-ss) if it was written after sunset.

Since the preceding conjunction of the moon took place Aug. 24.78 (= Aug. 24 at 6:43 P.M. Elephantine civil time, counted from midnight), the translation period amounted to .97 of a day (23 hours, 17 minutes) if Aug. 25/26 (ss-ss) was Elul 1, or 1.97 days (47 hours, 17 minutes) if Aug. 26/27 (ss-ss) was Elul 1. Not until all the various papyri have been discussed can we reach reasonable conclusions. Hence we have to defer making a decision as to which of the two dates mentioned was Elul 18.

AP 6. Kislev 18 = Thoth [17], year 21, the beginning of the reign of Artaxerxes I (464 B.C.)

The Egyptian day number is broken. Cowley suggested restoring it to 7 or to 14; Gutesmann and Hontheim

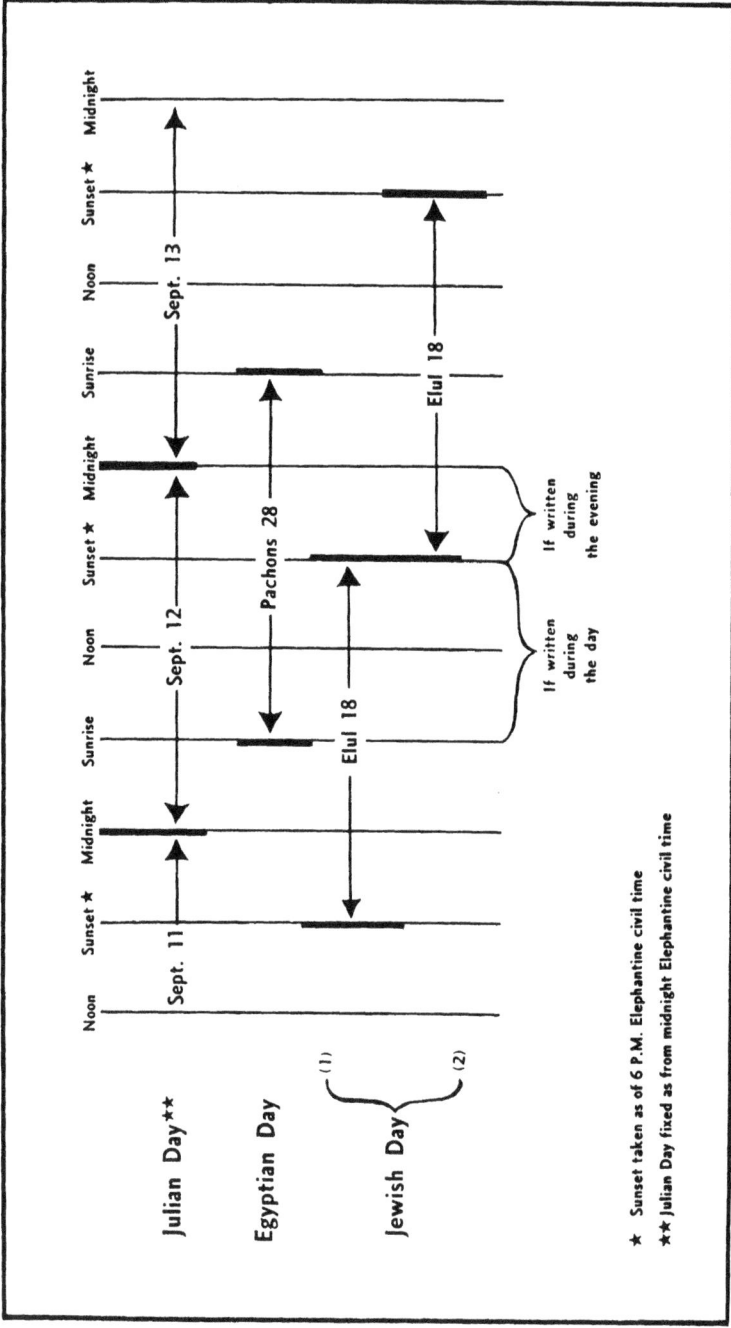

Fig. 9

The Differences in the Julian, Egyptian, and Jewish Days

The differences in the Julian, Egyptian, and Jewish days is shown, indicating that if a document was written during the Egyptian day Pachons 28, the corresponding Elul 18 could have been either the Jewish day that began at the preceding sunset or the day that began...

JEWISH CALENDAR AT ELEPHANTINE

restored it to 17.[19] No other restorations are paleographically possible. A ¾-inch break in the papyrus obliterates part of the number, leaving four vertical strokes. In this break the last two characters of the word יום "day" have to be supplied, since only the letter י is extant. The remaining gap is then about half an inch. It can be filled with three strokes, making the number 7. This actually gives paleographically the best picture as the reproduction on page 140 (Fig. 11-A) shows. The restoration of a "ten" in the gap does not fill it well (Fig. 11-B) and the figure 14 can therefore be disregarded. The insertion of the figure for 10 followed by 3 strokes, making the figure 17 (Fig. 11-C) is the only day number that can be made to agree astronomically with Kislev 18, but it must be admitted that the figure looks rather crowded, as Figure 11-C shows.

This papyrus is important, since it seems to equate the 21st year of one king with the beginning of the reign [20] of a King Artaxerxes. Since only Artaxerxes I succeeded to the throne in the 21st year of his predecessor (Xerxes), this latter king's name must be inferred.

In contrast to the usual method of the Jews in Elephantine, of giving only the Egyptian year if only one is mentioned, this is one of the two exceptional cases (also *Kraeling 6*) where only the Persian or Jewish year number is given instead.

The 21st year of Xerxes, which was also the accession

---

[19] Cowley, *op. cit.*, pp. 16, 17.

[20] The words *r's mlwkt'* (i.e. *r's mlkwt'*), here taken as designating the accession year, has been interpreted by Cowley (*op. cit.*, p. 15) and others as "1st year." This view is untenable for several reasons: (1) The phrase *r's mlkwt'*, "beginning of reign," is the exact Aramaic equivalent of the Akkadian accession-year formula *rēš sarrūti*, designating the time of reign before the beginning of the first full regnal year (Riekele Borger, *Babylonisch-Assyrische Lesestücke*, Heft 1 [Rome, 1963], Glossar, p. lxxvi); (2) for "year 1" a different phrase in Aramaic is used, *snt 1* (with the king's name) as in *Kraeling 9*, which is also the exact equivalent of the Akkadian date formula used in Babylonian texts; and (3) the explanatory but redundant clause translated by Cowley "when King Artaxerxes sat on his throne" can also be translated "when King Artaxerxes seated himself" or "was seated" on his throne, that is, "when he became king."

137

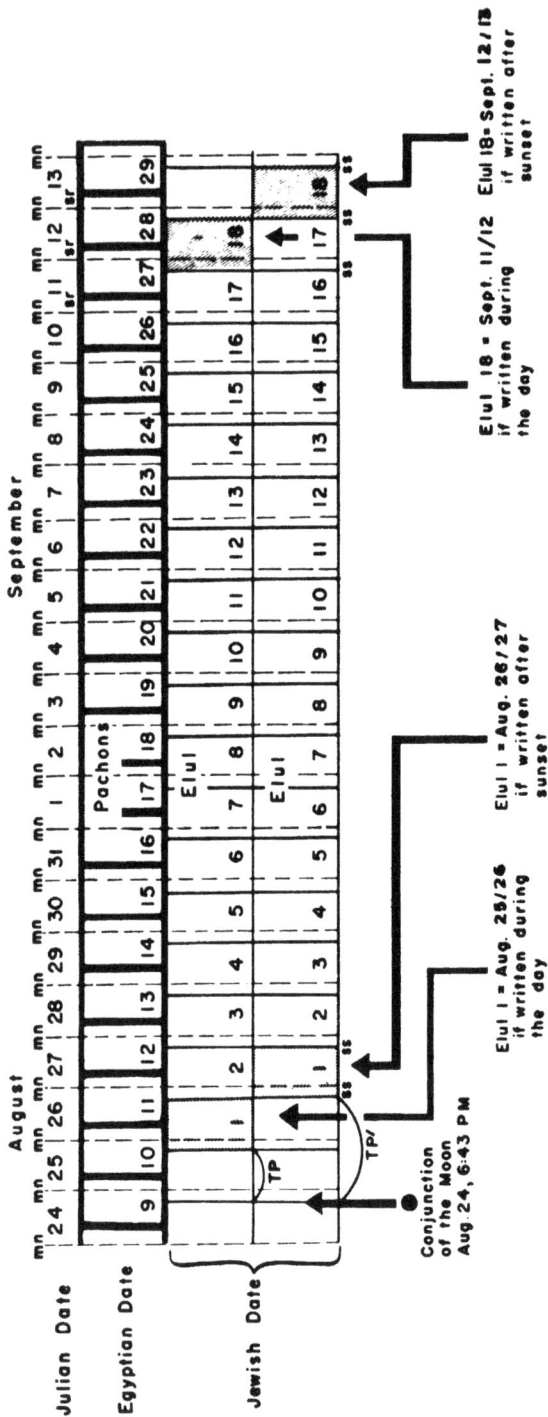

Julian Date

Egyptian Date

Jewish Date

August — September

Pachons — Elul — Elul

Conjunction of the Moon Aug. 24, 6:43 PM

KEY

mn = midnight to midnight
sr = sunrise to sunrise
ss = sunset to sunset
TP = translation period of 23 hrs. 17 min.
TP' = translation period of 47 hrs. 17 min.

Elul 1 = Aug. 25/26 if written during the day

Elul 1 = Aug. 26/27 if written after sunset

Elul 18 = Sept. 11/12 if written during the day

Elul 18 = Sept. 12/13 if written after sunset

Fig. 10

The Two Possible Dates for a Double-dated Papyrus Illustrated by Papyrus *AP 5*

Since the differences in day beginning between the Egyptian and Jewish days allow two theoretical possibilities for the placing of the Jewish day, the length of the translation period at the beginning of the month has to decide which scheme is most likely the correct one. The range of the translation period lies between 16½ and 42 hours, hence the first case, in which the translation period was 23 hrs. 17 min., is correct, and the document was written before sunset year of Artaxerxes I, began in the spring of 465 B.C. according to the Persian system of reckoning, and in the fall of the same year according to the Jewish civil year. The month Kislev, the 9th month of the Babylonian calendar, always fell toward the end of the Julian calendar year—thus from December, 465, to January, 464 B.C., during the year under discussion. The Egyptian month Thoth of that year began Dec. 17, 465, and ended Jan. 15, 464 B.C. That only Thoth 17 can be made to agree with Kislev 18 can be seen from the following results:

> Thoth 7 = Dec. 23/24 (sr-sr), 465 B.C.
> Thoth 14 = Dec. 30/31 (sr-sr), 465 B.C.
> Thoth 17 = Jan. 2/3 (sr-sr), 464 B.C.

The conjunction of the moon took place Dec. 15.04 (12:57 A.M.), 465 B.C. The earliest date possible for Kislev 1 would be Dec. 15/16 (ss-ss), 465 B.C., and the 18th of Kislev would then be Jan. 1/2 (ss-ss), 464 B.C.

If Kislev 1 was Dec. 15/16 (ss-ss), 465 B.C., the translation period amounted to .71 of a day (17 hours, 2 minutes); if Kislev 1 was Dec. 16/17 (ss-ss), the translation period would be 24 hours longer (41 hours, 2 minutes), and the document would have been written in the evening after sunset, since Kislev 18 would in that case have been Jan. 2/3 (ss-ss), 464 B.C.

Ap 8. Kislev 21 = Mesore 1, year 6 of Artaxerxes I

The papyrus is well preserved and creates no reading problems. However, the dates as given can be made to agree by no known methods, so that a scribal error must be involved. If the scribe mistakenly wrote Mesore 1 instead of a correct Mesore 21 the dates agree astronomically, though not with the Babylonian calendar. They are also in harmony if the month and day numbers are assumed to be correct, with the year 6 an error for year 5. But again no

A. Day Number Reconstructed to "7"

B. Day Number Reconstructed to "14"

C. Day Number Reconstructed to "17"

Fig. 11

The Break in the Date Line of Papyrus *AP 6* Reconstructed According to Three Possibilities

Since only one letter of the word "day" is preserved, the two missing characters of that word had to be put into each reconstruction. The three vertical strokes stand for the numeral three; the crescent-shaped sign is the numeral ten.

agreement would exist with the Babylonian calendar. The two possible results would be the following:

1. Kislev 21 = Mesore 1, year 5 (?) of Artaxerxes I (460 B.C.). Mesore 1 in the fifth of Artaxerxes I's Egyptian regnal years (288th year of the Nabonassar era) fell on Nov. 11/12 (sr-sr), 460 B.C. Kislev 21 would then have been either Nov. 10/11 (ss-ss) or Nov. 11/12 (ss-ss), and Kislev I either Oct. 21/22 (ss-ss) or Oct. 22/23 (ss-ss). Since the conjunction of the moon took place Oct. 21.09 (2:09 A.M.), the translation period would have amounted to .66 of a day (15 hours, 50 minutes) in the first case, and 1.66 days (39 hours, 50 minutes) in the second. However, it should be noticed that Kislev 1 was one lunar month later according to the Babylonian calendar.

2. Kislev 21 = Mesore 21 (?), year 6 of Artaxerxes I (459 B.C.). Mesore 21 in the 6th Egyptian year of Artaxerxes I fell on Dec. 1/2 (sr-sr), 459 B.C. Kislev 21 was therefore either Nov. 30/Dec. 1 (ss-ss) or Dec. 1/2 (ss-ss), 459 B.C., and Kislev 1 either Nov. 10/11 or Nov. 11/12 (ss-ss). The conjunction took place Nov. 9.14 (3:21 A.M.), and the translation period would have been 1.61 days (38 hours, 38 minutes) or 2.61 days (62 hours, 38 minutes). Again if the results were correct, Kislev would have been a whole month earlier than according to the Babylonian calendar.

If the date line of the papyrus needed no emendation to achieve an agreement with astronomical facts, we should have the proof here that the Jews of Elephantine had failed to observe the second Adar in harmony with the Babylonian year in 462 B.C., and had not inserted it during the years 461 and 460; in that case they were one lunar month behind the Babylonian calendar. Unfortunately, these results are gained through conjectural corrections of the date line of *AP 8,* which make them rather doubtful. If another mistake is involved, different from those two conjectures, the results may be different.

AP 9. Year 6 of Artaxerxes I

The document is related to *AP 8* and may have borne the same date, perhaps without a scribal error. The date line, however, is so badly preserved that no certain conclusions can be reached.

Cairo Sandstone Stele.[21] בירח Sivan = Mechir, year 7 of Artaxerxes I (458 B.C.)

Because of the wide range of this date and its ambiguity, this stele does not settle the problem raised by *AP 8*. If the 7th year of Artaxerxes is recorded here according to the Egyptian system of reckoning, as is most likely the case, it is the 290th year of the Nabonassar era, beginning Dec. 16, 459, and ending Dec. 15, 458 B.C. The month Mechir of the 7th year of Artaxerxes I as reckoned in the Egyptian calendar extended from May 15 through June 13, 458 B.C. The month Sivan according to the Babylonian calendar extended from June 6 through July 5, 458 B.C.,[22] or according to the hypothetical reconstruction of the Elephantine calendar based for those years on *AP 8* (in which the months of the Jewish calendar preceded those of the Babylonian calendar by one lunar month), from May 8 through June 5, 458 B.C.

If the word בירח of the inscription is to be read "in the month," it can fit both schemes, since Sivan 1-8 of the Babylonian calendar overlapped with the last 8 days of the Egyptian month Mechir, and Sivan 8-29 according to the hypothetical Jewish calendar based on *AP 8* overlapped with the first 22 days of Mechir also. If, however, בירח means "on the first day of the lunar month," [23] only a calendar in which the months coincided with the Babylonian months

---

[21] For the monument, see M. le Marquis Melchior de Vogüé, "Inscription araméenne trouvée en Egypte," *Comptes rendus des séances de L'Académie des Inscriptions et Belles-Lettres*, July 3, 1903, pp. 269-276, and Plate.

[22] Parker and Dubberstein, *Babylonian Chronology* (1956), p. 32.

[23] As Professor Kraeling suggested orally to S. H. Horn.

can be meant, since the first day of Sivan of the supposed Jewish calendar did not fall in Mechir.

Kraeling 14. Iyyar [8] = Tybi 20

In this badly broken marriage document the name and regnal-year number of the king are missing. Only five strokes of the day number of Iyyar are preserved. The preceding gap seems to allow a restoration to the number 8, the only possible date which agrees with Tybi 20 (well preserved) during the whole 5th century B.C.[24] A careful analysis of all years during the 5th century—the period in which these papyri were written—leads to the conclusion that Iyyar 8 agrees with Tybi 20 only five times, once during the reign of Darius I, in 496 B.C.; twice under Xerxes, in 482 and 471 B.C.; and twice during the reign of Artaxerxes I, in the years 457 and 446 B.C. It seems unnecessary to present the calendrical evidence for each one of these dates, since the fragmentary state of this document and the absence of a royal name do not permit a final conclusion for any of the five possible dates.

Kraeling 1. Phamenoth 25 = Sivan 20, year 14 of Arta-xerxes I (451 B.C.)

Although the scribe used an unusual sequence in this papyrus, giving the Egyptian month first—a method followed only once more, in Kraeling 6—the year number was, as in most cases, the Egyptian regnal year of Artaxerxes I, because no harmony between the dates could be achieved if year 14 was meant to be counted according to the Jewish reckoning. The reversed sequence must therefore be ascribed to a scribal slip.

Phamenoth 25 in Artaxerxes I's 14th Egyptian regnal year was July 6/7 (sr-sr), 451 B.C. Sivan was consequently

---

[24] A restoration of the number to 15 or 25 is impossible since Iyyar 15 or 25 never coincided with Tybi 20 during the 5th century B.C.

either July 5/6 (ss-ss) or July 6/7 (ss-ss). The conjunction of the moon took place June 16.59 (2:09 P.M.), giving a translation period of .16 of a day (3 hours, 50 minutes) if Sivan 1 was June 16/17 (ss-ss), or 1.16 days (27 hours, 50 minutes) if Sivan 1 was June 17/18 (ss-ss), 451 B.C.

Kraeling 2. [Tammuz] 18 = Pharmuthi [3], year 16 of Artaxerxes I (449 B.C.)

The Jewish month name and the Egyptian day number are broken away in the papyrus. They are restored here on the basis of calendrical computations, since Tammuz is the only Jewish month which has an 18th day that will synchronize with any day of the month Pharmuthi in the 16th Egyptian regnal year of Artaxerxes I. The day number 3 for Pharmuthi is restored because it gives the best translation periods. In view of some of the low translation periods of the previous papyri, Pharmuthi 2 as the correct Egyptian date cannot be ruled out entirely as impossible. The following statistics will show the different possibilities.

Pharmuthi 2 in the 16th Egyptian regnal year was July 12/13 (sr-sr), 449 B.C.; Pharmuthi 3 was July 13/14 (sr-sr). Tammuz 18 would have been one of the three possible dates, July 11/12, 12/13, or 13/14 (ss-ss). The conjunction of the moon took place June 23.92 (10:04 P.M.), and the translation period would have been .83 of a day (19 hours, 55 minutes) if Tammuz 1 was June 24/25, 1.83 days (43 hours, 55 minutes) if Tammuz 1 was June 25/26, and 2.83 days (67 hours, 55 minutes) if Tammuz 1 was June 26/27.

AP 13. Kislev 2 (?) = Mesore 11 (?), year 19 of Artaxerxes I (446 B.C.)

The reproduction of the papyrus[25] shows only two visible strokes of the day number for Kislev, and no room

---

[25] Sayce and Cowley, *op. cit.*, Plate containing "Papyrus E, 1-13."

for the third stroke that Cowley considers "probable." [26] Since Kislev 3 would give extremely low translation periods, Kislev 2—also read thus by Hontheim and allowed by Gutesmann as possible [27]—is most probably the correct Jewish date.

There are only faint traces of the figure that goes with the Egyptian month Mesore. Cowley, who had the original before him, read 10,[28] but from the published facsimile one could also read 11,[29] in which case the translation period for Kislev 2 would be reasonable, as the following will show.

Mesore 11 was Nov. 18/19 (sr-sr), 446 b.c., and Kislev 2 was consequently Nov. 17/18 (ss-ss) or Nov. 18/19 (ss-ss). Since the conjunction took place Nov. 16.25 (6:00 a.m.), the translation period was .50 of a day (12 hours) if Kislev 1 was Nov. 16/17 (ss-ss), 1.50 days (36 hours) if Kislev 1 was Nov. 17/18 (ss-ss).

AP 14. Ab 14 = Pachons 19, year 25 of Artaxerxes I (440 B.C.)

Pachons 19 in the 25th Egyptian year of Artaxerxes was Aug. 26/27 (sr-sr), 440 b.c., and Ab 14 either Aug. 25/26 (ss-ss) or Aug. 26/27 (ss-ss). The conjunction of the moon occurred Aug. 12.81 (7:26 p.m.). If Ab 1 was Aug. 12/13 (ss-ss), it would have begun even .06 of a day (1 hour, 26 minutes) *before* the actual conjunction took place, which is unthinkable. If Ab 1 was Aug. 13/14 (ss-ss), the translation period would have been of a more reasonable length, .94 of a day (22 hours, 33 minutes).

Kraeling 3. Elul 7 = Payni 9, year 28 of Artaxerxes I (437 B.C.)

Payni 9 in Artaxerxes' 28th Egyptian year was Sept. 14/15 (sr-sr), 437 b.c., and Elul 7 consequently either Sept. 13/

---

[26] Cowley, *op. cit.*, p. 38.
[27] *Ibid.*
[28] *Ibid.*
[29] Sayce and Cowley, *loc. cit.*

14 (ss-ss) or Sept. 14/15 (ss-ss). Since the conjunction occurred Sept. 7.55 (1:12 P.M.), the translation period would have been only .20 of a day (4 hours, 48 minutes) if Elul 1 was Sept. 7/8 (ss-ss), but the more reasonable length of 1.20 days (28 hours, 48 minutes) if Elul 1 fell on Sept. 8/9 (ss-ss).

AP 10. Kislev 7 = Thoth 4, year [2]9 of Artaxerxes I (437 B.C.?)

The papyrus is perfectly preserved and offers no reading difficulties. However, its year number 9 seems to be a mistake for 29 since in all the regnal years of Artaxerxes I Kislev 7 agrees with Thoth 4 only in his 4th[30] and 29th Egyptian years.

Thoth 4 in Artaxerxes' 29th Egyptian regnal year was Dec. 13/14 (sr-sr), 437 B.C., and therefore Kislev 7 either Dec. 12/13 (ss-ss) or Dec. 13/14 (ss-ss). The conjunction of the moon took place Dec. 5.74 (5:45 P.M.), and the translation period amounted to 1.01 days (24 hours, 14 minutes) if Kislev 1 was Dec. 6/7 (ss-ss), or 2.01 days (48 hours, 14 minutes) if Kislev 1 was Dec. 7/8 (ss-ss), 437 B.C.

If the year 29 is a correct reconstruction of the date of this papyrus, it was written in the same Julian calendar year as the preceding papyrus (*Kraeling 3*), although the regnal years differed, the 1st of Thoth being a turning point for the beginning of a new regnal year in Egypt. In this way they check one against the other. It is only unfortunate that the year number 29 is nothing more than a

---

[30] Since it is easier to assume that the scribe made a mistake by writing a 9 instead of a correct 29 for the year number, no consideration is given in the text to the other possibility that he wrote a mistaken 9 instead of the number 4. But for completeness' sake the computations for year 4 will be given here. Thoth 4 in the 4th Egyptian regnal year of Artaxerxes I was Dec. 20 (sr-sr), 462 B.C. Consequently Kislev 7 would have been either Dec. 19/20 (ss-ss) or Dec. 20/21 (ss-ss). Since the conjunction had occurred Dec. 12.53 (12:43 P.M.), the translation period would have amounted to 1.22 days (29 hours, 16 minutes) if Kislev 1 was Dec. 13/14 (ss-ss), or 2.22 days (53 hours, 16 minutes) if Kislev 1 was Dec. 14/15 (ss-ss).

conjecture, even though it is a conjecture that is based on good evidence.

AP 15. [Tishri 25] = Epiphi 6, year [30] of [Artaxerx]es I (435 B.C.?)

The first line, containing the date, is badly damaged. Epiphi 6 is preserved, but although the reading "Tishri 25" fits the poor remnants of some visible letters, it is far from certain that the reconstruction proposed here presents the correct or only possible reading. Nothing remains of the year number, and only the last letter remains of the king's name, which must have been Artaxerxes I, as the contents of the document show.[31] Although no weight can be placed on the results obtained from any computation about this papyrus, they are nevertheless presented here for the sake of completeness.

A near agreement between Tishri 25 and Epiphi 6 can be obtained only in the years 449 and 435 B.C. For the year 449 a check is provided now by *Kraeling 2*, which is unfortunately also a broken papyrus. To make both papyri fit, Pharmuthi 3 in *Kraeling 2* would have to be changed to Pharmuthi 2, and Tishri 25 in *AP 15* to Tishri 24.[32] Since the computations for the year 435 B.C. require no such changes, that year is most likely to be correct.

Epiphi 6 in 435 B.C. was Oct. 11/12 (sr-sr), and Tishri 25 consequently Oct. 10/11 (ss-ss) or Oct. 11/12 (ss-ss). The conjunction of the moon had taken place Sept. 15.44 (10:33 A.M.), so that the translation period amounted to 1.31 days (31 hours, 26 minutes) if Tishri 1 was Sept. 16/17

---

[31] Cowley, *op. cit.*, p. 44.

[32] There are 95 or 96 days in a lunar calendar from Tammuz 18 to Tishri 25, but only 93 from Pharmuthi 3 to Epiphi 6 in the Egyptian solar calendar. To make the two different intervals equal requires therefore a lengthening of one and a shortening of the other. From Pharmuthi 2 to Epiphi 6 are 94 days, and from Tammuz 18 to Tishri 24 are 94 or 95 days.

(ss-ss), but 2.31 days (55 hours, 26 minutes) if Tishri 1 was Sept. 17/18 (ss-ss).

Kraeling 4. Tishri 25 = Epiphi 25, year 31 of Artaxerxes I (434 B.C.)

Epiphi 25 in Artaxerxes' 31st Egyptian year was Oct. 30/31 (sr-sr), 434 B.C., and Tishri 25 either Oct. 29/30 (ss-ss) or Oct. 30/31 (ss-ss). The conjunction had taken place Oct. 4:37 (8:52 A.M.), and the translation period amounted therefore to 1.38 days (33 hours, 7 minutes) if Tishri 1 was Oct. 5/6 (ss-ss), or to 2.38 days (57 hours, 7 minutes) if Tishri 1 was Oct. 6/7 (ss-ss).

Kraeling 5. Sivan 20 = Phamenoth 7, year 38 of Artaxerxes 1 (427 B.C.)

Phamenoth 7 in the 38th Egyptian year of Artaxerxes was June 12/13 (sr-sr), 427 B.C. Since Sivan 20 was therefore either June 11/12 (ss-ss) or June 12/13 (ss-ss), and the conjunction of the moon had taken place May 22.21 (5:02 A.M.), the translation period amounted to 1.54 days (36 hours, 57 minutes) if Sivan 1 was May 23/24 (ss-ss), or 2.54 days (60 hours, 57 minutes) if Sivan 1 was May 24/25 (ss-ss).

Kraeling 6. Pharmuthi 8 = Tammuz 8, year 3 of Darius II (420 B.C.)

There is no need to repeat here what has been said concerning this papyrus on pp. 84-88, where it was shown that the dates of this document can be made to agree with each other only if year 3 means the 3d regnal year of Darius II according to a fall-to-fall Jewish calendar.

In the 3d regnal year of Darius II according to Jewish reckoning (but already in the 4th year according to Egyptian reckoning) Pharmuthi 8 was July 11/12 (sr-sr), 420 B.C. Tammuz was therefore either July 10/11 (ss-ss) or July 11/12 (ss-ss). The conjunction had occurred July 2.77

(6:28 P.M.), and the translation period amounted to .98 of a day (23 hours, 31 minutes) if Tammuz 1 was July 3/4 (ss-ss), or to 1.98 days (47 hours, 41 minutes) if Tammuz 1 was July 4/5 (ss-ss).

AP 20. בירח Elul = Pa[yni], year 4 of Darius II (420 B.C.)

Although only the first two letters of the word Payni are preserved in the papyrus, this reconstruction is certainly correct; a reconstruction to the alternative month Pha[ophi] is impossible, because Elul and Phaophi lay months apart during the whole 5th century B.C.

Payni 1 in the 4th regnal year of Darius II according to the Egyptian reckoning fell on Sept. 2/3 (sr-sr), 420 B.C. The nearest conjunction to this date occurred Aug. 31.12 (2:52 A.M.), and the 1st of Elul could probably have been counted Sept. 1/2 (ss-ss) with a translation period of 1.63 days (39 hours, 7 minutes), so that September 2 could have been called "first day of the month" if this meaning can be given to the word ירח. However, the traditional translation of בירח "in the month" also makes sense, since the two months are almost synchronous, and this document, the settlement of a claim, could have been written on almost any day of Elul to synchronize with the month of Payni.

Kraeling 7. בירח Tishri = Epiphi, year 4 of Darius II (420 B.C.)

This papyrus was written in the month following the one recorded in AP 20. Epiphi 1 was Oct. 2/3 (sr-sr), 420 B.C., and the 1st of Tishri was probably Sept. 30/Oct. 1 (ss-ss), since the conjunction had taken place Sept. 29.83 (7:55 P.M.), which would allow a translation period of .92 of a day (22 hours, 4 minutes). But Tishri 1 could also have been Oct. 1/2 (ss-ss), with a translation period of 1.92 days (46 hours, 4 minutes), so that once more an Egyptian

149

month began at approximately the same time as a Jewish month, and Epiphi 1 could have been called "the first" of Tishri, if such a translation for the word ירח is to be allowed.

Since this papyrus was written in Tishri after the beginning of a new Jewish civil year, and before the close of the Egyptian civil year, the regnal year 4 of Darius was the same according to each one of the three systems in use, as can be seen from Figure 4, on p. 86.

Kraeling 8. Tishri 6 = Payni 22, year 8 of Darius II (416 B.C.)

Inasmuch as the Egyptian month Payni synchronized with the month Elul in the 4th Egyptian year of Darius (*AP 20*), it is impossible for the same month to coincide with Tishri four years later. However, harmony can be achieved between Tishri 6 and Epiphi 22 in the 8th regnal year of Darius II. Hence it can be assumed that the scribe made a mistake in writing Payni instead of the next month Epiphi.

Epiphi 22 fell on Oct. 22/23 (sr-sr), 416 B.C., and Tishri 6 consequently on either Oct. 21/22 (ss-ss) or Oct. 22/23 (ss-ss). The conjunction had taken place Oct. 14.71 (5:02 P.M.), so that the translation period had a length of 2.04 days (48 hours, 57 minutes) if the 1st of Tishri was Oct. 16/17 (ss-ss). That Tishri 1 could have been Oct. 17/18 (ss-ss) is most unlikely, since the translation period in that case would have amounted to 3.04 days (72 hours, 57 minutes).

Another possibility would be to assume a mistake in the Jewish rather than the Egyptian month name, that is, to read Elul instead of Tishri. In that case Payni 22 would stand, which was Sept. 22/23 (sr-sr), 416 B.C., and Elul 6 would be either Sept. 21/22 (ss-ss) or Sept. 22/23 (ss-ss). The conjunction took place Sept. 15.23 (5:31 A.M.), allowing

a translation period of 1.52 days (36 hours, 28 minutes) if
Elul 1 was Sept. 16/17 (ss-ss), or of 2.52 days (60 hours, 28
minutes) if Elul 1 was Sept. 17/18 (ss-ss).

However, it is very unlikely that the scribe made the
mistake of writing Tishri instead of Elul, since Tishri
follows Elul, and it is very unusual to fall into the mistake
of confusing a future month with the current one. It is,
however, a common mistake to write the name of a past
month instead of the new one. This would have happened
here if the scribe mistakenly continued to write Payni
although he was already living in Epiphi, the next month.

AP 25. Kislev 3, year 8 = Thoth 12, year 9 of Darius II (416 B.C.)

This papyrus and the following are exceptionally important for the fact that they record the regnal year of
Darius according to both Jewish and Egyptian reckonings.
This was not done in all cases where the years actually
differ. [33]

Thoth 12 in the 9th Egyptian year of Darius II was
Dec. 16/17 (sr-sr), 416 B.C., and therefore Kislev 3 in either
the 8th Jewish or the 8th Persian year was Dec. 15/16
(ss-ss) or Dec. 16/17 (ss-ss). The conjunction of the moon
took place Dec. 12.98 (11:31 P.M.), which time allows a
translation period of .77 of a day (18 hours, 28 minutes) if
Kislev 1 was Dec. 13/14 (ss-ss), or of 1.77 days (42 hours,
28 minutes) if Kislev 1 was Dec. 14/15 (ss-ss).

AP 28. Shebat 24, year 13 = Athyr 9, year 14 of Darius II (410 B.C.)

Athyr 9 fell on Feb. 10/11 (sr-sr), 410 B.C., in the 14th
Egyptian regnal year of Darius II, which makes Shebat 24

---

[33] See the discussion on pp. 82, 83.

either Feb. 9/10 (ss-ss) or Feb. 10/11 (ss-ss). The conjunction took place Jan. 17.13 (3:07 A.M.), and the translation
period amounted to .62 of a day (14 hours, 52 minutes) if
the 1st of Shebat was Jan. 17/18 (ss-ss), or to 1.62 days (38
hours, 52 minutes) if Shebat 1 was Jan. 18/19 (ss-ss).

The two papyri last mentioned, *AP 25* and *AP 28*,
show clearly that the scribes who wrote these documents
employed different systems of reckoning the regnal years
of their Persian overlords, one according to the Egyptian
and the other according to the Jewish system. They were
not always consistent enough to mention both years, when
a difference existed, as in *AP 10* which mentions the same
Jewish and Egyptian months as *AP 25*, as has already been
discussed. [34]

Kraeling 9. Marcheshvan 24 = Mesore 29, year 1 of Arta-xerxes II (404 B.C.)

There are no contemporary tablets of the last three
years of Darius II, or of the accession year of Artaxerxes II.
Therefore we have heretofore depended on Ptolemy's
Canon and the Saros Tablet for fixing the first year of
Artaxerxes II.[35] The dates thus reached are now verified
and corroborated by this new double-dated papyrus and
the next one.

The first regnal year of Artaxerxes II according to
Ptolemy's Canon was the 344th year of the Nabonassar era,
beginning with Thoth 1 on Dec. 2, 405 B.C. Mesore 29 fell
therefore on Nov. 25/26 (sr-sr), 404 B.C., and Marcheshvan
24 was consequently either Nov. 24/25 (ss-ss) or Nov. 25/26
(ss-ss). The conjunction occurred Nov. 1.43 (10:19 A.M.)
and the translation period was therefore .32 of a day (7
hours, 40 minutes) if Marcheshvan 1 was Nov. 1/2 (ss-ss),

---

[34] See pp. 82, 83.
[35] Parker and Dubberstein, *Babylonian Chronology* (1956), pp. 18, 19.

or 1.32 days (31 hours, 40 minutes) if Marcheshvan 1 was Nov. 2/3 (ss-ss).

Kraeling 10. Adar 20 = Choiak 8, year 3 of Artaxerxes II (402 B.C.)

Choiak 8 of the 3d regnal year of Artaxerxes II according to Egyptian reckoning fell on March 9/10 (sr-sr), 402 B.C. Adar 20 was then either March 8/9 (ss-ss) or March 9/10 (ss-ss), and Adar 1 either Feb. 17/18 (ss-ss) with a translation period of .90 of a day (21 hours, 36 minutes) or Feb. 18/19 (ss-ss) with a translation period of 1.90 days (45 hours, 36 minutes), since the conjunction had taken place Feb. 16.85 (8:24 P.M.).

Conclusions

The results obtained from the study of the double-dated papyri are very instructive. However, not all the documents discussed so far can be used for a reconstruction of the Jewish calendar of the 5th century B.C.

Two of them, *AP 8* and *AP 10*, obviously contain errors, since their dates, as given, cannot be made to agree by any known method of computation. It is uncertain whether the corrections proposed above are sound, especially for *AP 8*, since the correction leads to conclusions that are at variance with a regular intercalation like that of the 19-year cycle.

Two other papyri, *Kraeling 14* and *AP 15*, are so badly broken that great parts of the date lines have been reconstructed without certainty that the reconstruction is correct. Since the conclusions reached in this way show once more a divergence from the 19-year cycle, it is safer not to rely on the results reached through reconstructed date lines.

Documents that contain no day number, as the *Cairo Sandstone Stele*, *AP 20*, and *Kraeling 7*, are valuable in supporting the over-all picture, but cannot be used for

No. of Papyrus	Year B.C.	EGYPTIAN DATE		Jewish month & day	JEWISH DATE			
					If written during day		If written after sunset	
		Egyptian month & day	Julian month & day		Julian month & day	Translation Period[a]	Julian month & day	Translation Period[a]
AP 5	471	Pach. 28	Sept. 12/13	Elul 18	Sept. 11/12	23 hrs. 17 min.	Sept. 12/13	47 hrs. 17 min.
AP 6	464	Tho. 17	Jan. 2/3	Kisl. 18	Jan. 1/2	17 " 2 "	Jan. 2/3	41 " 2 "
Kr 1	451	Pham. 25	July 6/7	Siv. 20	July 5/6	3 " 50 "	July 6/7	27 " 50 "
Kr 2	449	Phar. 3	July 13/14	Tam. 18	July 12/13	19 " 55 "	July 13/14	43 " 55 "
AP 13	446	Mes. 11	Nov. 18/19	Kisl. 2	Nov. 17/18	12 " 0 "	Nov. 18/19	36 " 0 "
AP 14	440	Pach. 19	Aug. 26/27	Ab 14	Aug. 25/26	(-1) " 26 ")b	Aug. 26/27	22 " 33 "
Kr 3	437	Pay. 9	Sept. 14/15	Elul 7	Sept. 13/14	4 " 48 "	Sept. 14/15	28 " 48 "
Kr 4	434	Epi. 25	Oct. 30/31	Tish. 25	Oct. 29/30	33 " 7 "	Oct. 30/31	57 " 7 "
Kr 5	427	Pham. 7	June 12/13	Siv. 20	June 11/12	36 " 57 "	June 12/13	60 " 57 "
Kr 6	420	Phar. 8	July 11/12	Tam. 8	July 10/11	23 " 31 "	July 11/12	47 " 31 "
AP 25	416	Tho. 12	Dec. 16/17	Kisl. 3	Dec. 15/16	18 " 28 "	Dec. 16/17	42 " 28 "
AP 28	410	Ath. 9	Feb. 10/11	Sheb. 24	Feb. 9/10	14 " 52 "	Feb. 10/11	38 " 52 "
Kr 9	404	Mes. 29	Nov. 25/26	Mar. 24	Nov. 24/25	7 " 40 "	Nov. 25/26	31 " 40 "
Kr 10	402	Choi. 8	March 9/10	Adar 20	March 8/9	21 " 36 "	March 9/10	45 " 36 "

◊ Dates resulting from a reasonable translation period.
[a] The time between the conjunction of the moon and the evening with which the first day of the month began.
[b] In this case the beginning of the month would have occurred 1 hr. 26 min. before conjunction; hence the minus sign.

Table 2

an exact reconstruction of the Jewish-calendar dating.

On the other hand, some broken documents have certainly been correctly reconstructed (*AP 6, Kraeling 2*), and the mistake in *Kraeling 8,* where the scribe evidently wrote an erroneous Payni instead of a correct Epiphi, can be easily detected. Hence it is valid to use these three last-mentioned documents as evidence in the conclusions to be reached below.

Table 2 offers a comparison of the results achieved from the study of the several papyri that can be used as reasonably trustworthy evidence. For each document the table presents the Egyptian date with its Julian equivalent; then it gives the Jewish month with the two possibilities of its Julian equivalent, the first date being correct if the document was written during the day, the second one if the document was written after sunset. The translation periods added indicate how much time elapsed from the conjunction of the moon until the evening of the day when the 1st of the month began. Dates resulting from a reasonable translation period are starred.

Table 2 shows that six dates arrived at from the 14 papyri will give reasonable translation periods only if one assumes that they were written after sunset; the other 8 could have been written during the hours of daytime.

The close harmony of the dates with the Babylonian calendar is striking. Since most translation periods are rather low, there is the possibility that the Jews in Elephantine did not entirely rely on the observation of the new crescent to determine the beginning of the new month. But the paucity of our source material makes it uncertain whether the Jews had developed, through a long period of experimentation and observation, a fixed calendar in which the number of days of each month had been calculated beforehand. The comparatively low translation periods can perhaps be explained by the fact that Elephantine

155

knows hardly any overcast sky, and therefore a new crescent can easily be observed as soon as it reaches the minimum elevation of visibility.

Unfortunately our papyri do not contain the names of any intercalary months, and we are not yet in a position to prove, as Jewish scholars have always maintained, that the Jews used only a second Adar, but never a second Elul. It seems plausible that they would have been reluctant to lengthen the interval between the great feasts of Nisan and those of Tishri.

However, one important aspect of these papyri is the proof that *Kraeling 6* gives of the existence of the civil fall-to-fall calendar among the 5th century Jews at Elephantine. Since this papyrus supports statements made in Nehemiah 1:1 and 2:1, implying the existence of such a calendar among postexilic Jewry, there is no reason left for doubt concerning the correctness of the date line of *Kraeling 6,* and the alternative assumption that a scribal error is involved must be rejected.

These papyri provide most welcome material for a reconstruction of some phases of the Jewish calendar of the pre-Christian era, for which no other source material is available except the meager information the Bible provides. Yet the small number of documents available as witnesses is far too scanty to arrive at unassailable conclusions as to every aspect of their lunar calendar.

However, the recent discovery of additional source material on which the foregoing conclusions have been based allows us to entertain reasonable hope that further data will fill the still existing gaps and permit a more complete reconstruction of the ancient Jewish calendar system.

RECONSTRUCTION OF THE JEWISH CALENDAR AT ELEPHANTINE

HOW TO USE THIS CALENDAR TABULATION:—Each horizontal line of dates in this tabulation represents a regnal year as reckoned in the Jewish fall-to-fall calendar, beginning with Tishri, the 7th month. The first eight-line section comprises the 14th through the 21st years of Xerxes, and the following sections are the reigns of Artaxerxes I and so on. The boldface figures are the B.C. years (those starred are leap years); and the dates on each line (10/6, 11/5, etc.) are the Julian-calendar dates on which the 1st of each Jewish month falls.

For example, the first line represents the 14th year of Xerxes by Jewish reckoning. It begins in 472 B.C. (second column) with Tish[ri] 1, which falls on October 6, abbreviated to 10/6 (third column), that is, the day beginning at sunset of October 5. The 1st of the next month, Mar[heshvan], is 11/5 (November 5, beginning at sunset of November 4); Kis[lev] 1 is December 4. Next comes the boldface figure 471, indicating the opening of a new B.C. year (Julian). Hence the remaining months of this Jewish year begin in 471: Teb[eth] 1 falls on January 3, 471; Sheb[at] 1 on February 1, Ad[ar] 1 on March 3, Nis[an] 1 on April 1. Iyy[ar] 1 on May 1, Siv[an] 1 on May 30, Tam[muz] 1 on June 29, Ab 1 on July 28, Elul 1 on August 27. This last date appears in a box because one of the double-dated papyri was written in that month, thus fixing the date. (The 14 dates so marked on this calendar are the basis on which the rest of the calendar is computed.)

In the next year, the 15th of Xerxes, which begins in 471 B.C. (September 25), Teb[eth] is still in 471; hence the boldface date 470 appears in the column between Tebeth and Shebat, which is the first month beginning in 470. This 15th year has a 13th month, the second Adar. The column headed "Ad[ar] II" shows that 7 out of 19 years contain the second Adar.

The Julian (B.C.) equivalents of the Jewish dates in this volume have been computed according to this tentative reconstruction of the Jewish calendar; for example, the dates of Ezra's journey to Judea (Ezra 7:9; 8:15, 31). In the tabulation the line numbered the 7th year of Artaxerxes I shows that year beginning by Jewish reckoning in 458 B.C., on Tishri 1 or October 2, and places Nisan 1 of that year, the date of Ezra's departure, on March 27, 457. Ezra left Ahava on the 12th of the same month, 11 days later, which would be April 7 (that is, April 6/7, sunset to sunset); and his arrival date, the 1st of the 5th month (Ab), was July 23. Although the B.C. number at the beginning of this 7th year is 458, it changes to 457 between Tebeth 1 and Shebat 1; hence Ezra's dates in Nisan and Ab are all in 457.

Year Regnal	BC	(7) Tish.	(8) Mar.	(9) Kis.	BC	(10) Teb.	BC	(11) Sheb.	(13) Ad. II	Ad.	(1) Nis.	(2) Iy.	(3) Siv.	(4) Tam.	(5) Ab	(6) Elul
XERXES																
14	472	10/6	11/5	12/4	471	1/3		2/1		3/3	4/1	5/1	5/30	6/29	7/28	[8/27]
15	471	9/25	10/25	11/23		12/23	470	1/21	3/22	2/20	4/20	5/20	6/18	7/18	8/16	9/15
16	470	10/14	11/13	12/12	469*	1/11		2/9		3/10	4/8	5/8	6/6	7/6	8/4	9/3
17	469	10/2	11/1	12/1		12/31	468	1/29		2/28	3/29	4/28	5/27	6/26	7/25	8/24
18	468	9/22	10/22	11/20		12/20	467	1/18	3/19	2/17	4/17	5/17	6/15	7/15	8/13	9/12
19	467	10/11	11/10	12/9	466	1/8		2/6		3/8	4/6	5/6	6/4	7/4	8/2	9/1
20	466	9/30	10/30	11/28		12/28	465*	1/26	3/26	2/25	4/24	5/24	6/22	7/22	8/20	9/19
21	465	10/18	11/17	[12/16]	464	1/15		2/13		3/15	4/13	5/13	6/11	7/11	8/9	9/8
ARTAXERXES I																
1	464	10/7	11/6	12/6	463	1/5		2/3		3/5	4/3	5/3	6/1	7/1	7/30	8/29
2	463	9/27	10/27	11/25		12/25	462	1/23	3/24	2/22	4/22	5/22	6/20	7/20	8/18	9/17
3	462	10/16	11/15	12/14	461*	1/13		2/11		3/12	4/10	5/10	6/8	7/8	8/6	9/5

(Dates shown in brackets — 8/27 in Elul of year 14, and 12/16 in Kislev of year 21 — appear in a box in the original.)

Year Regal BC	(7) Tish.	(8) Mar.	(9) Kis.	BC	(10) Teb.	BC	(11) Sheb.	(12) Ad.	(13) Ad. II	(1) Nis.	(2) Iyy.	(3) Siv.	(4) Tam.	(5) Ab	(6) Elul
4 461	10/4	11/3	12/2	460	1/1		1/30	3/1		3/30	4/29	5/28	6/27	7/26	8/25
5 460	9/23	10/23	11/21		12/21	459	1/19	2/18	3/20	4/18	5/18	6/16	7/16	8/14	9/13
6 459	10/12	11/11	12/11	458	1/10		2/8	3/10		4/8	5/8	6/6	7/6	8/4	9/3
7 458	10/2	11/1	11/30		12/30	457*	1/28	2/27		3/27	4/26	5/25	6/24	7/23	8/22
8 457	9/20	10/20	11/18		12/18	456	1/16	2/15	3/17	4/15	5/15	6/13	7/13	8/11	9/10
9 456	10/9	11/8	12/7	455	1/6		2/4	3/6		4/4	5/4	6/2	7/2	7/31	8/30
10 455	9/28	10/28	11/26		12/26	454	1/24	2/23	3/25	4/23	5/23	6/21	7/21	8/19	9/18
11 454	10/17	11/16	12/15	453*	1/14		2/12	3/13		4/11	5/11	6/9	7/9	8/7	9/6
12 453	10/5	11/4	12/4	452	1/3		2/1	3/3		4/1	5/1	5/30	6/29	7/28	8/27
13 452	9/25	10/25	11/23		12/23	451	1/21	2/20	3/22	4/20	5/20	6/18	7/18	8/16	9/15
14 451	10/14	11/13	12/12	450	1/11		2/9	3/11		4/9	5/9	6/7	7/7	8/5	9/4
15 450	10/3	11/2	12/2	449*	1/1		1/30	2/29		3/29	4/28	5/27	6/26	7/25	8/24
16 449	9/22	10/22	11/20		12/20	448	1/18	2/17	3/19	4/17	5/17	6/15	7/15	8/13	9/12
17 448	10/11	11/10	12/9	447	1/8		2/6	3/8		4/6	5/6	6/4	7/4	8/2	9/1
18 447	9/30	10/30	11/28		12/28	446	1/26	2/25		3/26	4/25	5/24	6/23	7/22	8/21
19 446	9/19	10/19	11/17		12/17	445*	1/15	2/14	3/15	4/13	5/13	6/11	7/11	8/9	9/8
20 445	10/7	11/6	12/5	444	1/4		2/2	3/4		4/2	5/2	5/31	6/30	7/29	8/28
21 444	9/26	10/26	11/24		12/24	443	1/22	2/21	3/23	4/21	5/21	6/19	7/19	8/17	9/16
22 443	10/15	11/14	12/14	442	1/13		2/11	3/13		4/11	5/11	6/9	7/9	8/7	9/6
23 442	10/5	11/4	12/3	441*	1/2		1/31	3/1		3/30	4/29	5/28	6/27	7/26	8/25
24 441	9/23	10/23	11/21		12/21	440	1/19	2/18	3/20	4/18	5/18	6/16	7/16	8/14	9/13
25 440	10/12	11/11	12/10	439	1/9		2/7	3/9		4/7	5/7	6/5	7/5	8/3	9/2
26 439	10/1	10/31	11/29		12/29	438	1/27	2/26	3/28	4/26	5/26	6/24	7/24	8/22	9/9
27 438	10/20	11/19	12/18	437*	1/17		2/15	3/16		4/14	5/14	6/12	7/12	8/10	8/30
28 437	10/8	11/7	12/7	436	1/6		2/4	3/6		4/4	5/4	6/2	7/2	7/31	8/30
29 436	9/28	10/28	11/26		12/26	435	1/24	2/23	3/25	4/23	5/23	6/21	7/21	8/19	9/18
30 435	10/17	11/16	12/15	434	1/14		2/12	3/14		4/12	5/12	6/10	7/10	8/8	9/7
31 434	10/6	11/5	12/5	433*	1/4		2/2	3/3		4/1	5/1	5/30	6/29	7/28	8/27
32 433	9/25	10/25	11/23		12/23	432	1/21	2/20	3/22	4/20	5/20	6/18	7/18	8/16	9/15
33 432	10/14	11/13	12/12	431	1/11		2/9	3/11		4/9	5/9	6/7	7/7	8/5	9/4
34 431	10/3	11/2	12/1		12/31	430	1/29	2/28		3/29	4/28	5/27	6/26	7/25	8/24
35 430															

Appendix 4

THE XERXES-ARTAXERXES TRANSITION

This appendix will furnish relevant excerpts from ancient historical narratives, and further information on other sources and authorities related to the contents of chapter 5.

A. Ancient Narratives

1. *Ctesias* (5th century B.C.).—The oldest narrative of the death of Xerxes and the accession of Artaxerxes is the following summary:

Artabanus, being very powerful with Xerxes, plotted with the equally powerful eunuch Aspamitres to assassinate Xerxes. They killed him and then convinced his son Artaxerxes that Darius, the other son, had killed him. But Darius, led by Artabanus, came to the house of Artaxerxes and denied with loud cries that he was the murderer of his father; but he was put to death.

Artaxerxes reigned with the support of Artabanus, but in turn became the object of his plotting. Artabanus associated with himself in this plot Megabyzus, who was already annoyed because he suspected his wife Amytis [sister of Artaxerxes] to be an adulteress. And they [Artabanus and Megabyzus] bound themselves together by mutual oaths. But Megabyzus revealed it all, and Artabanus was put to death in the same manner as he had intended to kill Artaxerxes. Everything that had been done to Xerxes and Darius now became clear, and Aspamitres died a cruel and miserable death for having been an accomplice in the murder of Xerxes and Darius. For he was put into the "boat" [enclosed between two tight-fitting troughs and left to die] and thus was killed. But there was a battle after the death of Artabanus between his fellow conspirators and the other Persians; the three sons of Artabanus were killed in this battle. Megabyzus was badly wounded; and Artaxerxes together with Amytis and Rhodogune and their mother Amestris lamented greatly. He was barely saved through the careful treatment of Apollinides, a physician from Cos.

160

Bactria and its satrap, another Artabanus, revolted against Artaxerxes, and there ensued a battle that ended indecisively. When it was resumed, the wind blew in the faces of the Bactrians so that Artaxerxes gained the victory with the result that Bactria submitted to him.[1]

There is no reason to doubt that the story in this summary of Ctesias' narrative, by Photius (9th century A.D.), transmits the principal facts as told in Ctesias' lost *Persica*, though it may ha ˌ omitted additional information that would have thrown light on some of the variations in other ancient accounts. It presumably represents the official story, as Ctesias learned it at the court of Artaxerxes I's grandson.

2. *Aristotle* (4th century B.C.).—In enumerating examples of attacks on rulers, Aristotle mentions this case:

For instance Artapanes [*sic*] killed Xerxes fearing the charge about Darius, because he had hanged him when Xerxes had ordered him not to but he had thought he would forgive him because he would forget, as he had been at dinner.[2]

This sort of incidental illustration, perhaps written from memory, can hardly be considered a serious historical source for the fact of Xerxes' assassination. The absurd implication that Xerxes was expected to overlook his son's murder further lowers the credibility of this statement that places Darius' death before that of Xerxes.

3. *Diodorus of Sicily* (late 1st century B.C.).—In his historical account Diodorus adds details not now found in Ctesias, such as Artabanus' attacking and being killed by Artaxerxes, and the latter's brother Hystaspes being absent.

With the passing of this year [465 B.C.], in Athens Lysitheüs was archon, and in Rome the consuls elected were Lucius Valerius Publicola and Titus Aemilius Mamercus. During this year, in Asia Artabanus, an Hyrcanian by birth, who enjoyed the greatest influence at the court of King Xerxes and was captain of the royal body-guard, decided to slay Xerxes and transfer the king-

---

[1] Translated from Ctesias *Persica* (summary by Photius) secs. 29-31 (R. Henry ed., pp. 33-35).
[2] Aristotle *The Politics* v. 8. 14, 1311b, 38 (Loeb ed., pp. 448, 449).

ship to himself. He communicated the plot to Mithridates the eunuch, who was the king's chamberlain and enjoyed his supreme confidence, and he, since he was also a relative of Artabanus as well as his friend, agreed to the plot. And Artabanus, being led at night by Mithridates into the king's bed-chamber, slew Xerxes and then set out after the king's sons. These were three in number, Darius the eldest and Artaxerxes, who were both living in the palace, and the third, Hystaspes, who happened to be away from home at the time, since he was administering the satrapy of Bactria. Now Artabanus, coming while it was yet night to Artaxerxes, told him that his brother Darius had murdered his father and was shifting the kingship to himself. He counselled him, therefore, before Darius should seize the throne, to see to it that he should not become a slave through sheer indifference but that he should ascend the throne after punishing the murderer of his father; and he promised to get the body-guard of the king to support him in the undertaking. Artaxerxes fell in with the advice and at once, with the help of the body-guard, slew his brother Darius. And when Artabanus saw how his plan was prospering, he called his own sons to his side and crying out that now was his time to win the kingship he strikes Artaxerxes with his sword. Artaxerxes, being wounded merely and not seriously hurt by the blow, held off Artabanus and dealing him a fatal blow killed him. Thus Artaxerxes, after being saved in this unexpected fashion and having taken vengeance upon the slayer of his father, took over the kingship of the Persians. So Xerxes died in the manner we have described, after having been king of the Persians for more than twenty years, and Artaxerxes succeeded to the kingship and ruled for forty years.

When Archedemides was archon in Athens, the Romans elected as consuls Aulus Verginius and Titus Minucius, and the Seventy-ninth Olympiad was celebrated, that in which Xenophon of Corinth won the "stadion" [464 B.C.]. . . .

When Tlepolemus was archon in Athens [463 B.C.], the Romans elected as consuls Titus Quinctius and Quintus Servilius Structus. This year Artaxerxes, the king of the Persians, who had just recovered the throne, first of all punished those who had had a part in the murder of his father and then organized the affairs of the kingdom to suit his own personal advantage. Thus with respect to the satraps then in office, those who were hostile to him he dismissed and from his friends he chose such as were

THE XERXES-ARTAXERXES TRANSITION

competent and gave the satrapies to them. He also concerned himself with both the revenues and the preparation of armaments, and since in general his administration of the entire kingdom was mild, he enjoyed the favour of the Persians to a high degree.[3]

4. *Trogus Pompeius, or Gnaeus Pompeius Trogus* (1st century B.C. to 1st century A.D.). — Trogus' history, as abridged by Justin (3d century A.D. or later), differs in some details from the accounts of Ctesias and Diodorus, though not necessarily contradicting either. It adds an account of how Artaxerxes lured Artabanus to his death.

Xerxes, king of Persia, once the terror of the nations around him, became, after his unsuccessful conduct of the war against Greece, an object of contempt even to his own subjects. Artabanus, his chief officer, conceiving hopes of usurping the throne, as the king's authority was every day declining, entered one evening into the palace (which from his intimacy with Xerxes was always open to him), accompanied by his seven stout sons, and, having put the king to death, proceeded to remove by stratagem such of the king's sons as opposed his wishes. Entertaining little apprehension from Artaxerxes, who was but a boy, he pretended that the king had been slain by Darius, who was of full age, that he might have possession of the throne the sooner, and instigated Artaxerxes to revenge parricide by fratricide. When they came to Darius's house, he was found asleep, and killed as if he merely counterfeited sleep. But seeing that one of the king's sons was still uninjured by his villa[i]ny, and fearing a struggle for the throne on the part of the nobles, he took into his councils a certain Bacabasus, who, content that the government should remain in the present family, disclosed the whole matter to Artaxerxes, acquainting him by what means his father had been killed, and how his brother had been murdered on a false suspicion of parricide; and, finally, how a plot was laid for himself. On this information, Artaxerxes, fearing the number of Artabanus's sons, gave orders for the troops to be ready under arms on the following day, as if he meant to ascertain their strength, and their respective efficiency for the field. Artabanus, accordingly, presenting himself under arms among the rest, the

---

[3] Diodorus Siculus xi. 69. 1-70.1; xi. 71. 1-3 (Loeb ed., vol. 4, pp. 304-307, 308-311).

163

king, pretending that his corslet was too short for him, desired Artabanus to make an exchange with him, and, while he was disarming himself, and defenceless, ran him through with his sword, ordering his sons, at the same time, to be apprehended. Thus this excellent youth at once took revenge for his father's murder, and saved himself from the machinations of Artabanus.[4]

5. *Cornelius Nepos* (1st century B.C. to 1st century A.D.). —In a brief mention of several Persian kings Nepos remarks on Xerxes' murder by Artabanus, a satrap, but throws no light on the circumstances:

But of those who were sovereigns with absolute authority, the most eminent were, as we think, Cyrus, king of the Persians, and Darius, the son of Hystaspes. . . . There are also three others of the same nation; Xerxes and the two Artaxerxes, Macrochir and Mnemon. . . . Of these, the two of the same name died a natural death; the third was killed with the sword by Artabanus, one of his satraps.[5]

Nepos refers to another event that has a bearing on the accession of Artaxerxes. He speaks of the visit of the Greek exile Themistocles to Artaxerxes (not Xerxes as some held).

I know most historians have related that Themistocles went over into Asia in the reign of Xerxes, but I give credence to Thucydides in preference to others, because he, of all who have left records of that period, was nearest in point of time to Themistocles, and was of the same city. Thucydides says that he went to Artaxerxes, and sent him a letter in these words: "I, Themistocles, am come to you, a man, who, of all the Greeks, brought most evil upon your house, when I was obliged to war against your father, and to defend my own country. I also did your father still greater service, after I myself was in safety, and he began to be in danger; for when he wished, after the battle fought at Salamis, to return into Asia, I informed him by letter that it was in contemplation that the bridge, which he had constructed over the Hellespont, should be broken up, and that he should be surrounded by enemies; by which information he was rescued from danger. But now, pursued by all Greece, I have fled to you, solicit-

---

[4] Trogus Pompeius (or Gnaeus Pompeius Trogus), abridged in Justinus Frontinus (also called Marcus Junianus Justinus), *History of the World, Extracted From Trogus Pompeius*, iii.1, in John Selby Watson trans., *Justin, Cornelius Nepos, and Eutropius*, pp. 37, 38.
[5] Cornelius Nepos *Lives* xxi ("Of Kings"). 1, in Watson, *op. cit.*, p. 413.

ing your favour, and if I shall obtain it, you will find me no less deserving as a friend than your father found me resolute as an enemy. I make this request, however, that with regard to the subjects on which I wish to discourse with you, you would grant me a year's delay, and when that time is past, permit me to approach you."

The king, admiring his greatness of mind, and wishing to have such a man attached to him, granted his request.[6]

6. *Plutarch* (2d century A.D.).—On the Themistocles story Plutarch agrees with Nepos that it was not Xerxes but Artaxerxes who received the Greek exile.

Now Thucydides and Charon of Lampsacus relate that Xerxes was dead, and that it was his son Artaxerxes[7] with whom Themistocles had his interview; but Ephorus and Dinon and Clitarchus and Heracleides and yet more besides have it that it was Xerxes to whom he came. With the chronological data Thucydides seems to me more in accord, although these are by no means securely established. Be that as it may, Themistocles, thus at the threshold of the dreadful ordeal, had audience first with Artabanus the Chiliarch, or Grand Vizier,[8] and said that he was a Hellene, and that he desired to have an audience with the King on matters which were of the highest importance and for which the monarch entertained the most lively concern.[9]

Thucydides (5th century B.C.), here cited as the authority for the time of Themistocles' arrival, places it at a time when Artaxerxes "had lately come to the throne."

Then proceeding into the interior with one of the Persians who dwelt on the coast, he [Themistocles] sent on a letter to King Artaxerxes son of Xerxes, who had lately come to the throne. And the letter ran as follows: "I, Themistocles, am come to you, who of all Hellenes did your house most harm so long as your father assailed me and I was constrained to defend myself, but still greater good by far when, his retreat being in progress, I was in security and he in dire peril. . . . And now I am here, having it in my power to do you great good, being pursued by the Hellenes on account of my friendship to you; and my desire is

---

[6] *Ibid.*, ii ("Themistocles"). 9, 10, pp. 321, 322.
[7] The son's name is obvious, but is inserted by the translator.
[8] The translator has added "or Grand Vizier" to explain "Chiliarch," which means "commander of a thousand."
[9] Plutarch *Themistocles* 27. 1, 2 (Loeb ed., *Plutarch's Lives*, vol. 2, pp. 72, 73).

to wait a year and then in person explain to you that for which I am come." [10]

7. *Aelian* (3d century A.D. or earlier).—The latest classical author mentioning the death of Xerxes names a different murderer, presumably Darius. But his brief statement, offered with no supporting evidence and differing from all the other narratives, may be a mere inaccuracy of a very late writer. Yet it may represent a tradition handed down by partisans of Artabanus. Referring to Xerxes, he says:

Then returning [from his defeat in Greece] the most disgraced of men, he died, slain in bed by his son. [11]

B. Ancient Chronologists

1. *Manetho* (3d century B.C.) epitomized.—In the Epitome of Manetho's history the king list of the 27th Dynasty (Persian kings ruling as pharaohs of Egypt) includes Artabanus with a seven-month reign:

"3. Xerxês the Great, for 21 years.
4. Artabanus, for 7 months.
5. Artaxerxês, for 41 years." [12]

2. *Ptolemy, or Claudius Ptolemaeus* (2d century A.D.).— Ptolemy's Canon gives for the 21st year of Xerxes and the 1st of Artaxerxes an Egyptian-calendar dating that is indisputably fixed at 466/65 and 465/64 B.C., December to December; but omits all kings reigning less than one year, hence throws no light on the problem of Artabanus. [13]

---

[10] Thucydides i. 137. 3, 4 (Loeb ed., vol. 1, pp. 232-235). Plutarch, *loc. cit.*, mentions Ephorus, Dinon, Clitarchus, Heracleides, and others who held that it was Xerxes, but he agrees with Thucydides and Charon of Lampsacus (both contemporary with Themistocles) that it was Artaxerxes, since the chronological data harmonize better with this view. Diodorus (xi. 56. 5 to 58. 3, Loeb ed., vol. 4, pp. 270-277) places Themistocles' visit in the reign of Xerxes.

[11] Translated from Claudius Aelianus *Varia Historia* xiii.3 (Hercher ed., p. 146). For a note on the significance of Aelian's statement, see p. 106, note 39.

[12] Manetho *Aegyptiaca* (*Epitome*), Fragment 70 (from Africanus, preserved by Syncellus), Loeb ed., pp. 174, 175. There is also a fragment of a 5th-century papyrus (*ibid.*, footnote 1 and facsimile on Pl. III), listing the same dynasty and including [Arta]banus between Xerxes and Artaxerxes. This text seems to be independent of Africanus, differing in details.

[13] On Ptolemy's Canon see above, pp. 40-43; for the canon itself, see p. 128.

THE XERXES-ARTAXERXES TRANSITION

3. *Chronologies Derived From Manetho.*—Manetho's recognition of Artabanus was followed by two Christian chronographers: (1) Africanus (3d century), whose work is preserved only in part by Eusebius and Syncellus, and (2) Eusebius (4th century).

Africanus, in addition to transmitting Manetho's king list of the Persian period, equates the 20th year of Artaxerxes with the 4th year of the 83d Olympiad (445/44 B.C.), which dates the accession in Olymp. 78.4 (465/64 B.C.).[14]

Eusebius' *Chronicle,* in both extant versions, dates the seven months of Artabanus and the accession of Artaxerxes I in the year 1552 from the birth of Abraham, with which year is aligned the beginning of the 79th Olympiad. Since the different versions, editions, and manuscripts of the *Chronicle* differ in the alignment of the various year reckonings in the parallel columns and in the placement of the notes of events, some modern writers have cited Eusebius as placing the Artabanus-Artaxerxes entry in Olympiad 78, year 4, others in the following year (Olymp. 79.1). However, this entry seems to belong to Olymp. 78.4, as a close examination of the construction of the *Chronicle* indicates.[15]

---

[14] Julius Africanus *Chronography* (Fragments), in *Ante-Nicene Fathers,* vol. 6, pp. 135, 137; see also in Eduard Meyer, *Forschungen zur alten Geschichte,* vol. 2, p. 487.

[15] Eusebius, *Chronici Canones,* Jerome's Latin version, J. K. Fotheringham, ed., p. 192; cf. Armenian version, *Chronicon Bipartitum,* J. B. Aucher, ed., pp. 208, 209.

In one column the years of Abraham (*Anni Abrahae*) form a continuous era throughout, with Hebrew, Greek, Persian, and other year reckonings running in parallel columns for shorter or longer periods. The Olympiad reckoning (which is counted from the games held in midsummer of 776 B.C.) begins with the Year of Abraham 1240, the Olympiad numbers being entered on a line with, slightly below, or on the next line below every fourth year from 1240 on. It is generally accepted that Eusebius used an autumn-to-autumn year in his Era of Abraham; consequently the year 1240 would have been 777/776 B.C., ending about three months after the beginning of the first Olympiad year. Then Olymp. 1.1 would have begun in that Year of Abraham 1240 but synchronized mostly with 1241. Similarly Olymp. 79.1 (78 Olympiads or 312 years later) must have begun in midsummer 464 B.C., in the Year of Abraham 1552 but only a few months before its end. Thus any event in that year 1552 that occurred between the fall of 465 and about July 464, would have taken place before Olymp. 79.1 began and hence in Olymp. 78.4.

167

C. Modern Interpretations of the Sources

The earliest pioneers of modern chronology began, in the 16th century, to construct a scheme based on Ptolemy's Canon and the Greek historians. They accepted Ptolemy as the foundation, but for the period of Artaxerxes they were divided into three schools of thought, with three methods of dating the years of that reign and therefore three different B.C. dates for the events of Ezra 7.

1. *The canon dating applied.*—Joseph J. Scaliger, the precursor of many other chronologists (1583), reckoned Artaxerxes' reign by Ptolemy's Canon. He dated the death of Xerxes in J.P. (Julian Period [16]) 4249, which is 465 B.C., and the beginning of Artaxerxes' reign, that is, his year 1, in J.P. 4250 (464 B.C.). He identified the latter's year 7 with J.P. 4256 (458 B.C.) and year 20 with J.P. 4269 (445 B.C.).[17]

2. *The canon date shifted.*—Archbishop James Ussher (1650) abandoned Ptolemy here to place Xerxes' death and Artaxerxes' accession nine years earlier, in 474 B.C. He considered the Greek historical data as requiring the visit of Themistocles to be reckoned some years earlier than the canon would indicate. Others followed him in shortening one reign and lengthening the other by nine years,[18] or alternatively followed Pétau, who retained the canon date for Xerxes' death but supposed a ten-year coregency.[19]

---

[16] See p. 30n.

[17] Joseph J. Scaliger, *Opus de Emendatione Temporum* (1629 ed.), book 5, p. 408; book 6, pp. 607, 600. This computation of the canon years (as Egyptian calendar years) is correct. Some twenty years earlier Johann Funck (1564) had accepted the canon for the reigns of Xerxes and Artaxerxes (but dated Ezra 7 in 457 B.C.). He tried to date the canon by the Olympiads, but because he placed the first Olympiad one year late his whole Nabonassar era dating scale ran one year late, and thus he did not use the correct canon dating (see his *Ausslegung des andern theils des Neundten Capitels Danielis*, fols. F₆v, G₆r, N₆v, and tables).

[18] James Ussher, *Annales Veteris Testamenti*, pp. 187, 188, 192, 195; in the English version, *Annals of the World*, pp. 131, 132, 135, 137.

[19] The theory of a supposed ten-year coregency had been set forth nearly thirty years earlier (1627) by Petavius (Denis Pétau) in his *De Doctrina Temporum*, x. 26, xii. 33 (1757 ed., vol. 2, pp. 110, 111, 262, 263); and his *Rationarium Temporum*, part 2, book 3, sec. 10 (1733 ed., vol. 2, pp. 189, 192).

Ussher's A.M. and B.C. dates, including his nine-year shift of Artaxerxes (i.e., 467 and 454 B.C., respectively, for the 7th and 20th years of the reign), were long used in Catholic Bibles, Douay Version, also in chronological tables printed in many editions of the K.J.V. However, Ussher's B.C. dates in the K.J.V. *margins,* from the time when they were introduced by Bishop William Lloyd, in 1701, were revised here to correct Ussher's shift of Artaxerxes, for Lloyd followed the canon dating.[20] In making this revision the marginal dates for the 7th and 20th years of Artaxerxes (Ezra 7 and Nehemiah 1 and 2) were placed only *twelve* years apart (457 and 445) instead of thirteen, and thus they appear to this day. That is why Ussher, who actually dated the events of Ezra 7 in 467 B.C., came to be cited as authority for 457 B.C.

3. *The canon date adjusted.*—Isaac Newton (1728) followed the canon but attempted to adjust Ptolemy's Egyptian-calendar years to the "actual" regnal years of Artaxerxes. Concluding that the reign began in August or September of 464, he dated Nisan of the 7th and 20th years (Ezra 7:7-9; Nehemiah 2:1) in the spring of 457 and 444, respectively. His reasoning was based on the following three assumptions, all of them now known from archeological evidence to be erroneous: (1) that Ptolemy's Canon always antedates the reigns, for which reason the death of Xerxes must be placed *after* Thoth 1 (Dec. 17), 465 (from which Ptolemy reckoned Artaxerxes' year 1); (2) that Artaxerxes could not become king until seven months after that because of Artabanus' intervening reign; and (3) that it was at some time after the summer solstice of 464 that Artaxerxes came to the throne, beginning his year 1 then and reckoning

---

[20] British and Foreign Bible Society, *Historical Catalogue of Printed Editions of Holy Scripture*, vol. 1, p. 248; for Lloyd's chronology of Artaxerxes, see his appendix in Benjamin Marshall, *Chronological Tables*, table IV, appendix, part 1, col. 5 (cf. table III, col. B).

each succeeding regnal year from the anniversary of his accession.[21]

4. *More recent historians.*—Modern historians have taken into account the chronological evidence of the cuneiform tablets, combined with the fragmentary stories of the Greek writers. They have usually ignored Artabanus as a factor in the chronology since he is not recognized in the tablet dating. But W. W. Tarn, apparently accepting the Manetho king list, says that Artabanus reigned for seven months and was recognized in Egypt, also that he defeated Hystaspes, the other son of Xerxes, before Artaxerxes was able to kill him and take over.[22] A. T. Olmstead, apparently from Trogus' description of Artaxerxes as a mere boy, calls him an eighteen-year-old when he came to the throne; he holds that Megabyzus was involved in the original plot against Xerxes and that Hystaspes headed the revolt of Bactria against Artaxerxes but was defeated after the death of Artabanus.[23]

D. Sources for Similar Double-Year Datings

The preceding sections of Appendix 4 have surveyed the historical and chronological sources and authorities related to the Xerxes-Artaxerxes transition. Also relevant to the interpretation of the only *contemporary* document (*AP 6,* dated in both reigns) are the parallel examples on cuneiform tablets and the evidence for the Egyptian reckoning of the regnal years.

1. *The Artaxerxes I-Darius II transition.*—Three cuneiform tablets at the end of Artaxerxes I's reign appear to indicate by their double dating (not in two calendars, but in two regnal years) that the scribes who wrote them were uncertain as to what reign they should date by.

---

[21] Isaac Newton, *The Chronology of Ancient Kingdoms Amended,* pp. 353-355; also his *Observations Upon the Prophecies,* pp. 130, 131, 142, 143.
[22] W. W. Tarn, in *Cambridge Ancient History,* vol. 4, p. 2.
[23] A. T. Olmstead, *History of the Persian Empire,* pp. 289, 290.

THE XERXES-ARTAXERXES TRANSITION

We shall not enter into the murky history of events which began with the death of Artaxerxes I and ended with the accession of Darius II, but briefly summarize the recorded sequence of happenings: At the death of Artaxerxes I his son Xerxes II occupied the throne for the brief period of 45 days. He was then killed by his half brother Secydianus (or Sogdianus), who thereupon became king for about seven months, and then in turn was killed by another half brother who reigned as Darius II.[24] The length of reigns of Xerxes II and Secydianus is not certain, because there are no contemporary records in existence which recognize either of these two men as kings, and it is quite possible that their combined reigns occupied less than the 8½ months assigned to them by the ancient historians.

The last-known tablet dated to Artaxerxes I comes from the 9th month of his year 41 (December, 424), unless there is one dated to the 11th month (February, 423). Furthermore, there are two tablets dated to Darius' accession year in the 11th month. On the other hand, there are two other tablets written in the 12th month and one unpublished text from even earlier—all three double dated in the last year of Artaxerxes and in the accession year of Darius.[25]

2. *The Kandalanu-Nabopolassar transition.*—Another exceptional dating is found in the Kandalanu-Nabopolassar transition, when Kandalanu's reign is even extended into the year after his death. This was the period when Nabopolassar wrested Babylonia from Assyria. The last-known Babylonian tablet dated to the reign of Kandalanu comes from the 2d month of his year 21. The next two tablets bearing his name in the date line were written in the

---

[24] Manetho, *loc. cit.;* Ctesias secs. 44-48 (Henry ed., pp. 43-46); cf. Diodorus Siculus xii. 64. 1, 71. 1 (Loeb ed., vol. 5, pp. 60, 61, 78, 79); Thucydides iv. 50. 3 (Loeb ed., vol. 2, pp. 298, 299).
[25] The various texts referred to in this paragraph are listed in Parker and Dubberstein, *Babylonian Chronology* (1956), p. 18.

8th month of *year 22* "after Kandalanu," evidently after his death. It was the year in which Nabopolassar took over Babylon, and which later was reckoned as an interregnum. A chronicle tablet actually speaks of this year as the year "after Kandalanu, in the accession year of Nabopolassar."[26]

That Nabopolassar won recognition as the new ruler even before his official accession to the throne is attested by several dated tablets. Such tablets come from the 2d and 6th months of his accession year, while he was still fighting for the throne, and during a time when the old regime was still carried on until the 8th month of that same year, as shown by the aforementioned documents dated in the 8th month "after Kandalanu"—evidently written by scribes who did not yet have faith in the new government.[27] It was only on the 26th of the 8th month (Nov. 23, 626) that Nabopolassar felt strong and secure enough to have his official coronation, which is described in the Babylonian chronicle thus: "Nabopolassar sat upon the throne in Babylon. (This was) the 'beginning of reign' of Nabopolassar."[28]

We thus find in the records variously dated in the accession year of Nabopolassar a rather close parallel to other documents that are double dated in the name of one king after his death and in the name of another king who had already come to the throne, but whose position was not yet secure enough to disperse all possible doubt that his reign would be permanent.

E. AP 6 and the Egyptian Calendar

It is a well-known fact that Xerxes' Egyptian year 21 began on Thoth 1 (December 18), 466. This is attested by the astronomically fixed canon of Ptolemy and a double-

---

[26] *Ibid.*, p. 11; Wiseman, *op. cit.*, pp. 89, 90.

[27] Parker and Dubberstein, *loc. cit.*

[28] Wiseman, *op. cit.*, p. 51. This exact date for the accession, not known until the discovery of the Babylonian chronicle, shows that Ptolemy's Canon postdated Nabopolassar's reign.

THE XERXES-ARTAXERXES TRANSITION

dated papyrus (*AP 5*) of Xerxes' 15th year. On Thoth 1 (Dec. 17), 465, the year number would have been changed to Xerxes' year 22, if he had been alive at that date. Yet 16 days later, Jan. 2, 464, *AP 6* is still dated in "year 21." [29]

It is equally certain that the Egyptian year 465/4, in which *AP 6* was written, was counted as the 1st year of Artaxerxes and not his accession year. This is attested, not only by Ptolemy's Canon, but also by several double-dated papyri dated in this reign (pp. 135-148). If Artaxerxes became king before Thoth 1 (Dec. 17), 465 (perhaps during the preceding month of August, if the tablet *LBART 1419*, written in the Hellenistic period, is correct), his accession year would end with that Egyptian-calendar year on December 16, 465, and his year 1 would begin on Thoth 1, the next day.

AP 6 was written as late as Thoth 17, but was still dated "accession year." If that was the Egyptian accession year,[30] it would indicate (1) that Artaxerxes could not have been recognized in Egypt as king before Thoth 1, else Thoth 17 would have been labeled as having fallen in his year 1, and (2) that this recognition must have come before Thoth 17, otherwise the king's name would not have appeared in

---

[29] See Fig. 6, p. 110.

[30] The usual method of Egyptian scribes was to "antedate" reigns, i.e., to begin dating a king's reign in "year 1" immediately after his accession, and to change to "year 2" at the following Egyptian New Year's Day.

R. A. Parker, however, believes that the Egyptians while under Persian rule called the interval between a King's accession and the next Thoth "year 1" only if the king came to the throne between Thoth 1 and Nisan 1, but that if the king came to the throne in the period between Nisan 1 and Thoth 1, the Egyptians used the principle of the accession year, the postdating method, after the Persian model, in order to keep the Egyptian year beginning always on the Thoth 1 preceding the corresponding Persian year, which began on Nisan 1. See his "Persian and Egyptian Chronology," *AJSL*, 58 (1941). pp. 298-301; and "Some Considerations on the Nature of the Fifth-Century Jewish Calendar at Elephantine," *JNES*, 14 (1955), p. 271. Parker's reasoning, as developed in his first-mentioned article, is plausible, but its correctness cannot be proved by contemporary evidence. For the subject discussed here, this matter is unimportant.

This postdating method would have applied to Artaxerxes in the case discussed above if he had come to the throne in August, 465. But even so Thoth 17 (Jan. 2/3), 464, the date of *AP 6*, would no longer be in Artaxerxes' accession year, but in "year 1."

the dateline at all. This leads to a further conclusion. If this was Artaxerxes' accession year according to Egyptian reckoning, his year 1 would not have begun earlier than Thoth 1 (Dec. 17), 464. This would conflict with all known Egyptian source material according to which Artaxerxes' 2d regnal year began in Egypt December 17, 464.

Even the assumption that the 7-month reign of Artabanus, as recorded in the Manetho Epitome, entered into the Egyptian dating, does not help, because there are less than five months between August, in which according to the Hellenistic tablet Xerxes had been murdered, and the January date of *AP 6*. Furthermore, such a reign of Artabanus, with the consequent delay in beginning the reign of Artaxerxes, would have required the scribes to change the numbering of Artaxerxes' regnal years afterward, because the later attested numbering assigns his Egyptian year 1 to 465/64. There is no evidence for such a change, nor is such a procedure known in any other case. For these reasons the possibility that a 7-month reign of Artabanus delayed the dating of Artaxerxes' reign in the Egyptian calendar must be rejected.

It can therefore confidently be asserted that the expressions "year 21" and "accession year of Artaxerxes" in *AP 6* cannot refer to a reckoning in the Egyptian calendar. This means, then, that the two expressions must refer to a Semitic calendar, either the Babylonian-Persian calendar beginning with the spring month of Nisanu, or the Jewish calendar beginning with the autumn month of Tishri.

How the double reckoning of *AP 6* works out in the Persian and Jewish calendars has been shown by the second and third bands of Figure 6, p. 110, where the year in which Xerxes died and Artaxerxes I came to the throne is encased by heavy lines in both these calendars. Thence the later years in both reckonings (Fig. 7, p. 116) can be computed.

Bibliography

ADCOCK, F. E. "Caesar's Dictatorship," *The Cambridge Ancient History*, vol. 9. Edited by S. A. Cook, F. E. Adcock, and M. P. Charlesworth. Cambridge: The University Press, 1932. Pp. 691-740.

ADENEY. See *The Expositor's Bible.*

AELIANUS, CLAUDIUS. *Varia Historia.* Edited by Rudolf Hercher. Leipzig: B. G. Teubner, 1887. 209 pp.

AFRICANUS, JULIUS. *Chronography* (Fragments). *The Ante-Nicene Fathers*, vol. 6. Edited by A. Roberts and J. Donaldson. Grand Rapids, Mich.: Wm. B. Eerdmans Publishing Co., 1957. Pp. 130-138.

ALBRIGHT, WILLIAM FOXWELL. *From the Stone Age to Christianity.* 2d ed. Baltimore: The Johns Hopkins Press, 1946. 367 pp.

————. "The Gezer Calendar," *Bulletin of the American Schools of Oriental Research*, no. 92 (December 1943), pp. 16-26.

————. "The Nebuchadnezzar and Neriglissar Chronicles," *ibid.*, no. 143 (October, 1956), pp. 28-33.

The American Ephemeris and Nautical Almanac. (Annual) Washington: Government Printing Office 1852- .

ARCHER, PETER. *The Christian Calendar and the Gregorian Reform.* New York: Fordham University Press, 1941. 124 pp.

ARISTOTLE. *The Politics*, with an English translation by H. Rackham. "The Loeb Classical Library." London: William Heinemann, Limited, 1932. 684 pp.

BELLELI, L[AZARE]. *An Independent Examination of the Assuan and Elephantine Aramaic Papyri.* London: Luzac & Co., 1909. 204 pp.

BICKERSTETH, EDWARD. *A Practical Guide to the Prophecies.* Reprinted from the 6th London ed. Philadelphia: Orrin Rogers, 1841. 312 pp.

BÖHL, FRANZ M. TH. Review of Gustaf Dalman, *Arbeit und Sitte in Palästina*, vols. 1, 2 (Gütersloh: C. Bertelsmann, 1928-32), *Archiv für Orientforschung*, 8 (1932-33), pp. 245, 246.

BORGER, RIEKELE. *Babylonisch-assyrische Lesestücke*, Heft 1.

175

Rome: Pontifical Biblical Institute, 1963. 89 pp.

BOWMAN, RAYMOND A. "Arameans, Aramaic, and the Bible," *Journal of Near Eastern Studies,* 7 (1948), pp. 65-90.

BRIGGS. See Brown.

BRITISH AND FOREIGN BIBLE SOCIETY. *Historical Catalogue of Printed Editions of Holy Scripture.* 2 vols. in 4. New York: Kraus Reprint Corporation, 1963.

BROWN, FRANCIS, DRIVER, S. R., and BRIGGS, CHARLES A. *A Hebrew and English Lexicon of the Old Testament . . . Based on the Lexicon of William Gesenius.* Oxford: The Clarendon Press, 1907. 1127 pp.

BUHL, FRANTS. *Wilhelm Gesenius' hebräisches und aramäisches Handwörterbuch über das Alte Testament.* Reprint of the 17th ed. Berlin: Springer-Verlag, 1949. 1013 pp.

CARY. See Gardner.

CASSIUS DIO COCCEIANUS. *Dio's Roman History,* with an English translation by Ernest Cary on the basis of the version of Herbert Baldwin Foster. 9 vols. "The Loeb Classical Library." London: William Heinemann, Limited, 1914-1927.

CENSORINUS. *De Die Natale ("The Natal Day").* Translated by William Maude. New York: The Cambridge Encyclopedia Co., 1900. 40 pp.

CHABOT, J.-B. "Les papyri araméens d'Éléphantine sont-ils faux?" *Journal Asiatique,* 10th series, 14 (1909), pp. 515-522.

CHAMBERS, GEORGE F. *A Handbook of Descriptive and Practical Astronomy.* 4th ed. Vol. 2: Oxford: The Clarendon Press, 1890.

Chronographus Anni CCCLIIII, in *Chronica Minora Saec. IV. V. VI. VII.,* vol. 1. Edited by Theodor Mommsen. "Monumenta Germaniae Historica," Auct. Ant., vol. 9. Berlin: Weidmann, 1892. Pp. 13-196.

CLERKE, AGNES MARY. "Astronomy: History of Astronomy," *Encyclopaedia Britannica,* vol. 2 (1945), pp. 581-590.

Commentary . . . by Bishops and Other Clergy. See *Holy Bible.*

COOK, S. A. "Chronology: II. The Old Testament," *The Cambridge Ancient History,* vol. 1. Edited by J. B.

BIBLIOGRAPHY

Bury, S. A. Cook, and F. E. Adcock. New York: The Macmillan Company, 1928. Pp. 156-166.

COWLEY, A. *Aramaic Papyri of the Fifth Century B.C.* Oxford: The Clarendon Press, 1923. 319 pp.

————, SAYCE and. See Sayce.

CROLY, GEORGE. *The Apocalypse of St. John.* 2d ed., rev. London: C. & J. Rivington, 1828. 470 pp.

CROSS, FRANK M., JR. "The Discovery of the Samaria Papyri," *The Biblical Archaeologist,* 26 (1963), pp. 110-121.

CTESIAS. *Persica,* in his *La Perse, L'Inde; Sommaires de Photius.* Edited by R. Henry. Brussels: J. Lebègue & Cie, 1947. 99 pp.

CUNINGHAME, WILLIAM. *A Dissertation on the Seals and Trumpets of the Apocalypse, and the Prophetical Period of the Twelve Hundred and Sixty Years.* 3d ed., rev. London: Thomas Cadell, 1832. 523 pp.

CURTIS, EDWARD LEWIS, and MADSEN, ALBERT ALONZO. *A Critical and Exegetical Commentary on the Books of Chronicles.* "The International Critical Commentary." New York: Charles Scribner's Sons, 1910. 534 pp.

DELITZSCH. See Keil.

DINSMOOR, WILLIAM BELL. *The Archons of Athens in the Hellenistic Age.* Cambridge, Mass.: Harvard University Press, 1931. 567 pp.

DIO CASSIUS. See Cassius Dio.

DIODORUS SICULUS. *Diodorus of Sicily,* with an English translation by C. H. Oldfather and others. 12 vols. (11 vols. completed). "The Loeb Classical Library." London: William Heinemann, Limited, 1933-.

DIONYSIUS EXIGUUS. *Liber de Paschale,* in *Dionysii Exigui [et al.] . . . Opera Omnia.* "Patrologia Latina," vol. 67. Edited by J.-P. Migne. Paris: J.-P. Migne, 1865. Cols. 493-508.

DRIVER. See Brown.

DUBBERSTEIN. See Parker.

DUGAN. See Russell.

EUSEBIUS PAMPHILI. *Chronici Canones.* Translated into Latin by Jerome. Edited by J. K. Fotheringham. London: Humphrey Milford, 1923. 352 pp.

————. *Chronicon Bipartitum.* Armenian version with

Latin translation. Edited by J. B. Aucher. 2 vols. Venice: Mechitarist Fathers, 1818.

The Expositor's Bible. Edited by W. Robertson Nicoll. 26 vols. Vol. [7], *Ezra, Nehemiah, and Esther,* by Walter F. Adeney. New York: A. C. Armstrong and Son, 1908.

FABER, GEORGE STANLEY. *A Dissertation on the Prophecies . . . Relative to the Great Period of 1260 Years.* 2 vols. London: F. C. and J. Rivington, 1806.

FERGUSON, JAMES. *An Astronomical Lecture, on Eclipses of the Sun and Moon, the True Year of Our Saviour's Crucifixion, the Supernatural Darkness at That Time, and the Prophet Daniel's Seventy Weeks.* Bristol: S. Farley, [1775].

————. *Ferguson's Astronomy, Explained Upon Sir Isaac Newton's Principles.* With notes, and supplementary chapters by David Brewster. 2 vols. Edinburgh: John Ballantyne and Co., 1811.

————. *Tables and Tracts, Relative to Several Arts and Sciences.* London: A. Millar and T. Cadell, 1767. 328 pp.

Fessenden & Co.'s Encyclopedia of Religious Knowledge. Edited by J[ohn] Newton Brown. Brattleboro', Vt.: Brattleboro' Typographic Company, 1838. 1275 pp.

FIGULLA, H. H. *Ur Excavations; Texts, IV: Business Documents of the New-Babylonian Period.* Publications of the Joint Expedition of the British Museum and of the University Museum of Pennsylvania. London: The Trustees of the Two Museums, 1949. 69 pp. and 65 plates.

FOTHERINGHAM, J. K. "Calendar Dates in the Aramaic Papyri from Assuan," *Monthly Notices of the Royal Astronomical Society,* 69 (1908-1909), pp. 12-20.

————. "Note on the Regnal Years in the Elephantine Papyri," *ibid.,* pp. 446-448.

————. "A Reply to Professor Ginzel on the Calendar Dates in the Elephantine Papyri," *ibid.,* 71 (1911), pp. 661-663.

FREEDMAN, DAVID NOEL, "The Babylonian Chronicle," *The Biblical Archaeologist,* 19 (1956), pp. 50-60.

FREEMAN, DOUGLAS SOUTHALL. *George Washington: A*

BIBLIOGRAPHY

Biography. 7 vols. New York: Charles Scribner's Sons, 1948-1957.

FROOM, LEROY E. *The Prophetic Faith of Our Fathers.* Vol. 3. Washington: Review and Herald, 1946.

FUERST, JULIUS. *A Hebrew and Chaldee Lexicon to the Old Testament.* 3d ed., rev. Translated by Samuel Davidson. Leipzig: Bernhard Tauchnitz, 1867. 1511 pp.

FUNCK, JOHANN. *Ausslegung des andern theils des Neundten Capitels Danielis.* Königsberg: Johann Daubmann, 1564.

GARDINER, ALAN H. *Egyptian Grammar.* 3d ed., rev. Oxford: The Clarendon Press, 1957. 646 pp.

GARDNER, E. A., and CARY, M. "Early Athens," *The Cambridge Ancient History,* vol. 3. Edited by J. B. Bury, S. A. Cook, and F. E. Adcock. Cambridge: The University Press, 1929. Pp. 571-597.

GELLIUS, AULUS. *The Attic Nights of Aulus Gellius,* with an English translation by John C. Rolfe. Vol. 1. "The Loeb Classical Library." London: William Heinemann, Limited, 1927.

GERARD, JOHN. "Chronology," *The Catholic Encyclopedia,* vol. 3 (1908), pp. 738-742.

GESENIUS. See Brown; Buhl; Tregelles.

GINZEL, F[RIFDRICH] K[ARL]. *Handbuch der mathematischen und technischen Chronologie.* 3 vols. Leipzig: J. C. Hinrichs'sche Buchhandlung, 1906-1914.

——————. *Spezieller Kanon der Sonnen- und Mondfinsternisse.* Berlin: Mayer & Müller. 1899. 258 pp.

GNAEUS POMPEIUS TROGUS (Trogus Pompeius). See *Justinus Frontinus.*

GUTESMANN, S. "Sur le calendrier en usage chez les Israélites au Ve siècle avant notre ère," *Revue des études juives,* 53 (1907), pp. 194-200.

[HALE, APOLLOS]. "Diagram Exhibiting the Events of Prophecy," and later correction, *The Advent Herald,* 7 (1844), pp. 23, 77.

HALES, WILLIAM. *A New Analysis of Chronology and Geography, History and Prophecy.* 2d ed. 4 vols. London: C. J. G. & F. Rivington, 1830.

HARRIS, ZELLIG. *A Grammar of the Phoenician Language.* Vol. 8 of "American Oriental Series." Edited by W.

179

Norman Brown and others. New Haven, Conn.: American Oriental Society, 1936.

HATCH, WILLIAM HENRY PAINE. *An Album of Dated Syriac Manuscripts.* Boston, Mass.: The American Academy of Arts and Sciences, 1946. 286 pp.

Haydn's Dictionary of Dates. 17th ed. Edited by Benjamin Vincent. New York: Harper & Brothers, 1883. 796 pp.

Die Heilige Schrift des Alten Testaments. Edited by E. Kautzsch. 4th ed. 2 vols. Tübingen: J. C. B. Mohr, 1922, 1923.

HICKS, FREDERICK C. *Materials and Methods of Legal Research.* 3d rev. ed. Rochester, N.Y.: The Lawyers Cooperative Publishing Company, 1942. 659 pp.

HÖLSCHER. See *Heilige Schrift.*

The Holy Bible . . . With an Explanatory and Critical Commentary . . . by Bishops and Other Clergy of the Anglican Church. Edited by F. C. Cook. 12 vols. Vol. *3, II Kings-Esther,* by George Rawlinson. New impression. London: John Murray, 1900.

HONROTH, W., RUBENSOHN, O., and ZUCKER, F. "Bericht über die Ausgrabungen auf Elephantine in den Jahren 1906-1908," *Zeitschrift für ägyptische Sprache,* 46 (1909-1910), pp. 10-61.

HONTHEIM, P. J. "Die neuentdeckten jüd.-aram. Papyri von Assuan," *Biblische Zeitschrift,* 5 (1907), pp. 225-234.

HORN, SIEGFRIED H. "The Babylonian Chronicle and the Ancient Calendar of the Kingdom of Judah," *Andrews University Seminary Studies,* 5 (1967), pp. 12-27.

————, and WOOD, LYNN H. "The Fifth-Century Jewish Calendar at Elephantine," *Journal of Near Eastern Studies,* 13 (1954), pp. 1-20.

HUBER, PETER. Review of *Late Babylonian Astronomical and Related Texts,* edited by A. J. Sachs (Providence, R.I.: Brown University Press, 1955), *Bibliotheca Orientalis,* 13 (1956), pp. 231, 232.

International Critical Commentary. See Curtis; Skinner.

JONES, CHARLES W. "Development of the Latin Ecclesiastical Calendar," introduction to his edition of *Bedae Opera de Temporibus.* Cambridge, Mass.: The

Mediaeval Academy of America, 1943. Pp. 1-122.

JONES, H. STUART. "The Sources for the Tradition of Early Roman History," *The Cambridge Ancient History*, vol. 7. Edited by S. A. Cook, F. E. Adcock, and M. P. Charlesworth. Cambridge: The University Press, 1928. Pp. 312-332.

————, and LAST, HUGH. "The Early Republic," *ibid.*, pp. 436-384.

JOSEPHUS, FLAVIUS. *Josephus*, with an English translation by H. St. J. Thackeray (and others). 9 vols. "The Loeb Classical Library." Cambridge, Mass.: Harvard University Press, 1926-1965.

JUSTINUS FRONTINUS. *Justin's History of the World. Extracted From Trogus Pompeius*, in John Selby Watson, trans., *Justin, Cornelius Nepos, and Eutropius*. London: Henry G. Bohn, 1853. Pp. 17-304.

KALISCH, M. M. *A Historical and Critical Commentary on the Old Testament. . . . Genesis.* London: Longman, Brown, Green, Longmans, and Roberts, 1858. 780 pp.

KAUTZSCH. See *Heilige Schrift.*

KEIL, C. F., and DELITZSCH, F. *Biblical Commentary on the Old Testament.* 26 vols. Edinburgh: T. and T. Clark, 1857-1876.

KITTEL, RUD[OLF]. *Geschichte des Volkes Israel.* Vol. 3. Stuttgart: W. Kohlhammer, [1929].

KNOBEL, E. B. "Note on the Regnal years in the Aramaic Papyri from Assuan," *Monthly Notices of the Royal Astronomical Society*, 69 (1908-1909), pp. 8-11.

————. "A Suggested Explanation of the Ancient Jewish Calendar Dates in the Aramaic Papyri Translated by Professor A. H. Sayce and Mr. A. E. Cowley," *ibid.*, 68 (1907-1908), pp. 344-345.

KRAELING, EMIL G. *The Brooklyn Museum Aramaic Papyri.* New York: The Brooklyn Museum, 1953. 319 pp.

————. "New Light on the Elephantine Colony," *The Biblical Archaeologist*, 15 (1952), pp. 50-67.

KUGLER, FRANZ X. *Sternkunde und Sterndienst in Babel.* 3 vols. Münster: Aschendorffsche Verlagsbuchhandlung, 1907-1935.

LANGDON, S[TEPHEN]. *Babylonian Menologies and the Se-*

mitic Calendars. London: Humphrey Milford, 1935. 169 pp.

LANGE, JOHN PETER, and others. *A Commentary on the Holy Scriptures.* Translated and edited by Philip Schaff and others. [25] vols. New York: Charles Scribner's Sons, 1865-1915.

LAST. See Jones, H. Stuart.

LEHMANN, C. F., and GINZEL, F. K. "Die babylonisch-assyrischen Finsternisse," in F. K. Ginzel, *Spezieller Kanon der Sonnen- und Mondfinsternisse,* division 5, part 3, pp. 235-262. Berlin: Mayer & Müller, 1899.

[LLOYD, WILLIAM], Bishop of Worcester. Appendix, in Benjamin Marshall, *Chronological Tables.* Oxford: The Theater, 1713. Unpaged.

LODS, ADOLPHE. *Israel From Its Beginnings to the Middle of the Eighth Century.* Translated by S. H. Hooke. London: Kegan Paul, Trench, Trubner, & Co., Limited, 1932. 512 pp.

LUCKENBILL, DANIEL D. *Ancient Records of Assyria and Babylonia.* 2 vols. Chicago: The University of Chicago Press, 1926, 1927.

MADSEN. See Curtis.

MAHLER, ED[UARD]. "Die Doppeldaten der aramäischen Papyri von Assuan," *Zeitschrift für Assyriologie,* 26 (1912), pp. 61-76.

————. *Handbuch der jüdischen Chronologie.* Leipzig: Gustav Fock, 1916. 635 pp.

MALAMAT, A. "A New Record of Nebuchadnezzar's Palestinian Campaigns," *Israel Exploration Journal,* 6 (1956), pp. 246-256.

MANETHO. *Aegyptiaca (Epitome),* in *Manetho,* with an English translation by W. G. Waddell. "The Loeb Classical Library." Cambridge, Mass.: Harvard University Press, 1956. Pp. 3-187.

MARSHALL, BENJAMIN. See Lloyd.

MERCER, SAMUEL A. B. *Sumero-Babylonian Year-Formulae.* London: Luzac & Company, 1946. 121 pp.

MEYER, EDUARD. "Aegyptische Chronologie," *Abhandlungen der Königlichen Preussischen Akademie der Wissenschaften,* Berlin, 1904, Phil.-Hist. Klasse, part 1, pp. 1-212.

BIBLIOGRAPHY

————. *Forschungen der alten Geschichte.* 2 vols. Hildesheim: Georg Olms, 1966. [Reprint of 1892-1899 edition.]

————. "Nachträge zur ägyptischen Chronologie," *Abhandlungen der Königlichen Preussischen Akademie der Wissenschaften,* Berlin, 1907, Phil.-Hist. Klasse, part 3, pp. 1-46.

MILLER, WILLIAM. *Evidence From Scirpture* [sic] *and History of the Second Coming of Christ, About the Year 1843.* Troy [N.Y.]: Kemble & Hooper, 1836. 233 pp.

The Mishnah. Translated by Herbert Danby. London: Oxford University Press, 1944. 844 pp.

MORGENSTERN, JULIAN. "The New Year for Kings," in *Occident and Orient: Gaster Anniversary Volume.* London: Taylor's Foreign Press, 1936. 570 pp.

NEPOS, CORNELIUS. *Lives of Eminent Commanders,* in John Selby Watson, trans., *Justin, Cornelius Nepos, and Eutropius.* London: Henry G. Bohn, 1853. Pp. 305-450.

NEUFFER, JULIA. "The Accession of Artaxerxes I," *Andrews University Seminary Studies,* 6 (1968), pp. 60-87.

NEUGEBAUER, OTTO. *Astronomical Cuneiform Texts . . . of the Seleucid Period.* 3 vols. London: Lund Humphries, 1955.

————. "Die Bedeutungslosigkeit der 'Sothisperiode' für die älteste ägyptische Chronologie," *Acta Orientalia* 17 (1938), pp. 169-195.

————. *The Exact Sciences in Antiquity.* 2d ed. Providence, R.I.: Brown University Press, 1957. 240 pp.

————. "The Origin of the Egyptian Calendar," *Journal of Near Eastern Studies,* 1 (1942), pp. 396-403.

NEUGEBAUER, PAUL V., and WEIDNER, ERNST F. "Ein astronomischer Beobachtungstext aus dem 37. Jahre Nebukadnezars II. (-567/66)," *Berichte über die Verhandlungen der Königl. Sächsischen Gesellschaft der Wissenschaften zu Leipzig,* Phil.-Hist. Klasse, 67 (1915), part 2, pp. 28-89.

NEWTON, ISAAC. *The Chronology of Ancient Kingdoms Amended.* London: J. Tonson, J. Osborn, and T. Longman, 1728. 376 pp.

————. *Observations Upon the Prophecies.* London: J. Darby and T. Browne, 1733. 323 pp.

NEWTON, THOMAS. *Dissertations on the Prophecies.* Northampton, Mass.: William Butler, 1796. 591 pp.

NICHOL, FRANCIS D. *The Midnight Cry.* Christian Home Library ed. Washington: Review and Herald Publishing Association, 1944. 576 pp.

NOTH, MARTIN. "Die Einnahme von Jerusalem im Jahre 597 v. Chr.," *Zeitschrift des Deutschen Palästina Vereins,* 74 (1958), pp. 133-157.

OESTERLEY, W. O. E., and ROBINSON, THEODORE H. *A History of Israel.* 2 vols. Oxford: The Clarendon Press, 1934.

OLMSTEAD, A. T. *History of the Persian Empire.* Chicago: The University of Chicago Press, 1948. 576 pp.

OPPOLZER, THEODOR VON. *Canon der Finsternisse.* "Denkschriften der kaiserlichen Akademie der Wissenschaften," Math.-Naturwissensch. Klasse, vol. 52. Vienna: K. K. Hof- und Staatsdruckerei, 1887. 376 pp., 160 tables.

————. *Syzygien-Tafeln für den Mond.* "Publikation der astronomischen Gesellschaft," 16. Leipzig: Wilhelm Engelmann, 1881. 48 + 53 pp.

PARKER, RICHARD A. *The Calendars of Ancient Egypt.* "Studies in Ancient Oriental Civilization," no. 26. Chicago: The University of Chicago Press, 1950. 83 pp.

————. "Persian and Egyptian Chronology," *The American Journal of Semitic Languages and Literatures,* 58 (1941), pp. 285-301.

————. "Some Considerations on the Nature of the Fifth-Century Jewish Calendar at Elephantine," *Journal of Near Eastern Studies,* 14 (1955), pp. 271-274.

PARKER, RICHARD A., and DUBBERSTEIN, WALDO H. *Babylonian Chronology, 626 B.C.-A.D. 45.* "Studies in Ancient Oriental Civilization," no. 24, 2d ed. Chicago: The University of Chicago Press, 1946. 46 pp.

PARKER and DUBBERSTEIN, *Babylonian Chronology, 626 B.C.-A.D. 75.* "Brown University Studies," vol. 19. Providence, R.I.: Brown University Press, 1956. 47 pp.

PETAU, DENIS. *De Doctrina Temporum.* 3 vols. Venice: Bartholomaeus Baronchelli, 1757.

————. *Rationarium Temporum.* 3 vols. in 2. Venice: Laurentius Basilius, 1733.

BIBLIOGRAPHY

PFEIFFER, ROBERT H. *Introduction to the Old Testament.* 2d ed. New York: Harper & Brothers, 1948. 909 pp.

PINCHES, T. G. See Sachs.

PLINY (PLINIUS SECUNDUS). *Natural History,* with an English translation by H. Rackham (and others). 10 vols. "The Loeb Classical Library." Cambridge, Mass.: Harvard University Press, 1938-1962.

PLUTARCH. *Moralia,* with an English translation by Frank Cole Babbitt (and others). 15 vols. "The Loeb Classical Library." Cambridge, Mass.: Harvard University Press. In progress.

————. *Plutarch's Lives,* with an English translation by Bernadotte Perrin. 11 vols. "The Loeb Classical Library." Cambridge, Mass.: Harvard University Press, 1915-1926.

POEBEL, ARNO. "The Duration of the Reign of Smerdis, the Magian, and the Reigns of Nebuchadnezzar III and Nebuchadnezzar IV," *The American Journal of Semitic Languages and Literatures,* 56 (1939), pp. 121-145.

POGNON, H. "Chronologie des papyrus araméens d'Éléphantine," *Journal Asiatique,* 10th series, vol. 18 (1911), pp. 337-365.

POOLE, REGINALD L. *Medieval Reckonings of Time.* London: Society for Promoting Christian Knowledge, 1935. 47 pp.

PRITCHARD, JAMES B. ed. *Ancient Near Eastern Texts Relating to the Old Testament,* 2d ed. Princeton, N.J.: Princeton University Press, 1955. 544 pp.

PTOLEMY (CLAUDIUS PTOLEMAEUS). The *Almagest.* Translated by R. Catesby Taliaferro. "Great Books of the Western World," vol. 16. Edited by John Maynard Hutchins and Mortimer J. Adler. Chicago: Encyclopaedia Britannica, Inc., 1952. Pp. VII-XIV, 1-478.

The Pulpit Commentary. Edited by H. D. M. Spence and Joseph S. Exell. New ed. 52 vols. London: Funk & Wagnalls Company, [n.d.].

RAWLINSON. See *Holy Bible.*

ROBINSON. See Oesterley.

ROSE, H. J. "Calendar: Greek, Roman," *Encyclopaedia Britannica,* vol. 4 (1945), pp. 578, 579.

185

ROWLEY, H. H. *The Servant of the Lord and Other Essays on the Old Testament.* Oxford: Basil Blackwell, 1965. 355 pp.

RUBENSOHN. See Honroth.

RUDOLPH, WILHELM. *Esra und Nehemia. Handbuch zum Alten Testament,* Erste Reihe, 20. Tübingen: Verlag J. C. B. Mohr (Paul Siebeck), 1949. 22 pp.

RUSSELL, HENRY NORRIS, DUGAN, RAYMOND SMITH, STEWART, JOHN QUINCY. *Astronomy: A Revision of Young's Manual of Astronomy.* 2 vols. Boston: Ginn and Company, 1945.

SACHAU, EDUARD. *Aramäische Papyrus und Ostraka aus einer jüdischen Militär-Kolonie zu Elephantine.* Leipzig: J. C. Hinrichs'sche Buchhandlung, 1911. 290 pp. and facsimiles.

SACHS, A. J. ed. *Late Babylonian Astronomical and Related Texts.* Copied by T. G. Pinches and J. N. Strassmaier. Providence, R.I.: Brown University Press, 1955. 271 pp.

SAYCE, A. H., and COWLEY, A. E. *Aramaic Papyri Discovered at Assuan.* London: Alexander Moring, Ltd., 1906. 79 pp. and facsimiles of the papyri.

SCALIGER, JOSEPH. *Opus de Emendatione Temporum.* Rev. ed. Geneva: Typis Roverianis, 1629. 784 pp.

SCHÜRER, E. Review of *Aramaic Papyri Discovered at Assuan,* edited by A. H. Sayce with the assistance of A. E. Cowley (London, A. Moring, 1906), *Theologische Literaturzeitung,* 32 (1907). cols. 1-7.

————. "Der jüdische Kalender nach den aramäischen Papyri von Assuan. Nachtrag zu der Anzeige in Nr. 1," *ibid.,* cols. 65-69.

SIDERSKY, D. "Le calendrier sémitique des papyri araméens d'Assouan," *Journal Asiatique,* series 10, vol. 16 (1910), pp. 587-592.

SKINNER, JOHN. *A Critical and Exegetical Commentary on Genesis.* "The International Critical Commentary." New York: Charles Scribner's Sons, 1910. 551 pp.

SLOTKI. See *Soncino Books of the Bible.*

SMITH, SIDNEY. "The Age of Ashurbanipal," *The Cambridge Ancient History,* vol. 3. Edited by J. B. Bury, S. A. Cook, and F. E. Adcock. Cambridge: The University Press, 1929. Pp. 88-112.

BIBLIOGRAPHY

————. "The Foundation of the Assyrian Empire," *ibid.,* pp. 1-31.

SMYLY, J. GILBART. "An Examination of the Dates of the Assouan Aramaic Papyri," *Proceedings of the Royal Irish Academy,* vol. 27, sec. C (1908-1909), pp. 235-250.

SNOW, S. S. "Prophetic Time," *The Advent Herald,* 7 (1844), pp. 68, 69.

Soncino Books of the Bible. Edited by A. Cohen. 14 vols. Vol. [12], *Daniel, Ezra, and Nehemiah,* by Judah Slotki. London: The Soncino Press, 1951.

SPRENGLING, M[ARTIN]. "Chronological Notes for the Aramaic Papyri," *The American Journal of Semitic Languages and Literatures,* 27 (1911), pp. 233-266.

STRASSMAIER, J. N. "Einige chronologische Daten aus astronomischen Rechnungen," *Zeitschrift für Assyriologie,* 7 (1892), pp. 197-204.

————. "Zur Chronologie der Seleuciden," *ibid.,* 8 (1893), pp. 106-113.

————. *Inschriften von Cambyses, König von Babylon.* Parts 8, 9 of "Babylonische Texte." 12 parts. Leipzig: Verlag von Eduard Pfeiffer, 1890.

————, T. G. PINCHES and. See Sachs.

Talmud, The Babylonian. [Soncino English Translation.] Edited by I. Epstein. 34 vols. London: Soncino Press, 1935-1948.

TARN, W. W. "Persia, From Xerxes to Alexander," *Cambridge Ancient History,* vol. 6. Edited by J. B. Bury, S. A. Cook, and F. E. Adcock. Cambridge: The University Press, 1933. Pp. 1-24.

THATCHER, G. W. *Arabic Grammar.* 4th ed. London: Lund Humphries & Co., Ltd., 1942. 461 + 99 pp.

THIELE, EDWIN R. *The Mysterious Numbers of the Hebrew Kings.* Rev. ed. Grand Rapids, Mich.: William B. Eerdmans Publishing Co., 1965. 232 pp.

THUCYDIDES. [*History*], with an English translation by Charles Forster Smith. 4 vols. "The Loeb Classical Library." London: William Heinemann, Limited, 1930-1935.

TORREY, C. C. "Sanballat 'the Horonite,' " *Journal of Biblical Literature,* 47 (1928), pp. 380-389.

TREGELLES, SAMUEL PRIDEAUX. *Gesenius's Hebrew and*

Chaldee Lexicon to the Old Testament Scriptures. New York: John Wiley & Sons, 1905. 584 + 35 pp.

TROGUS POMPEIUS. See Justinus Frontinus.

UNGNAD, [ARTHUR]. "Eponymen," *Reallexikon der Assyriologie,* vol. 2 (1938), pp. 412-457.

USSHER, JAMES. *Annales Veteris Testamenti.* London: J. Flesher, 1650. 554 pp.

————. *Annals of the World.* London: E. Tyler, 1658. 907 pp.

VOGÜÉ, [MELCHOIR] de. "Inscription araméenne trouvée en Égypte," *Comptes rendus des séances de l'Académie des Inscriptions et Belles-Lettres,* July 3, 1903, pp. 269-276, and Plate.

WADE-GERY, H. T. "Chronological Notes," part 3, *The Cambridge Ancient History,* vol. 3. Edited by J. B. Bury, S. A. Cook, and F. E. Adcock. Cambridge: The University Press, 1929. Pp. 762-764.

WATSON, JOHN SELBY, trans. *Justin, Cornelius Nepos, and Eutropius.* London: Henry G. Bohn, 1853. 551 pp.

WEIDNER, ERNST. "Der altassyrische Kalender," *Archiv für Orientforschung,* 5 (1928-1929), pp. 184-185.

————. "Aus den Tagen eines assyrischen Schattenkönigs," *ibid.,* 10 (1935-1936), pp. 1-52.

————. "Zur altbabylonischen Jahresbenennung," *Orientalistische Literaturzeitung,* 15 (1912), cols. 392, 393.

————, NEUGEBAUER and. See Neugebauer, Paul V.

WELLHAUSEN, JULIUS. *Prolegomena to the History of Israel.* Translated by J. S. Black and Allan Menzies. Edinburgh: Adam & Charles Black, 1885. 552 pp.

WISEMAN, D. J. *Chronicles of Chaldaean Kings (626-556 B.C.) in the British Museum.* London: The British Museum, 1956. 99 pp.

WOOD, LYNN H. "The Kahun Papyrus and the Date of the Twelfth Dynasty (With a Chart)," *Bulletin of the American Schools of Oriental Research,* no. 99 (October, 1945), pp. 5-9.

————, HORN and. See Horn.

ZUCKER. See Honroth.

Index

Figures in italics indicate illustrations or tables

189

We invite you to view the complete
selection of titles we publish at:
www.TEACHServices.com

scan with your mobile
device to go directly
to our website

Please write or email us your praises, reactions, or
thoughts about this or any other book we publish at:

TEACH Services, Inc.
P U B L I S H I N G
www.TEACHServices.com • (800) 367-1844

11 Quartermaster Circle
Fort Oglethorpe, GA 30742

Info@TEACHServices.com

TEACH Services, Inc., titles may be purchased in bulk
for educational, business, fund-raising, or sales
promotional use. For information, please e-mail:

BulkSales@TEACHServices.com

Finally if you are interested in seeing
your own book in print, please contact us at

publishing@TEACHServices.com

We would be happy to review your manuscript for free.